Straight Talk
from Claudia Black

Straight Talk from Claudia Black

What Recovering Parents Should Tell
Their Kids about Drugs and Alcohol

Claudia Black, Ph.D.

 HAZELDEN®

Hazelden
Center City, Minnesota 55012-0176

1-800-328-0094
1-651-213-4590 (Fax)
www.hazelden.org

Library of Congress Cataloging-in-Publication Data
Black, Claudia.
  Straight talk from Claudia Black : what recovering parents should tell their
kids about drugs and alcohol / Claudia Black.
    p. cm.
    Includes bibliographical references.
    ISBN 1-59285-041-3 (paperback)
    1. Drug abuse.   2. Alcoholism.   3. Parents—Drug use.   4. Parents—Alcohol
use.   5. Alcoholics—Family relationships.   I. Title.
    HV5801.B549 2003
    362.29—dc21
                                                                2003050831

07 06 05 04   6 5 4 3 2

Cover design by David Spohn
Interior design by Rachel Holscher
Typesetting by Stanton Publication Services, Inc.

To Katie and Sean, my niece and nephew,
two very special young people in my life.

Contents

Acknowledgments

My thanks to several special friends and colleagues. This book is a better book because of all of you. As they say, the whole is bigger than the sum of its parts.

Wally Mitchell, your sharing so personally of yourself as a recovering father inspired me to take a turn with this book that I believe will be of inspiration to other parents too. The intimate sharing of Connie H., Clint W., Connie C., Mark S., Jean C., Sue R., Greg B., and Sandy N. added greatly to the heart of this book.

Mary Carol Melton, Sis Wenger, Sue Renes, Jean Collins, and Jerry Moe were most gracious in reading what was very rough material and then offering me extremely thoughtful feedback. I am appreciative and grateful.

Sandi Klein, my assistant, has been unwavering in her diligence to crafting my message. This has been one of many projects in the past several years, and the teamwork is most appreciated.

Rebecca Post, my editor at Hazelden Publishing, this has been a new working relationship that I have enjoyed greatly. I thank you and Hazelden Publishing for the opportunity to create *Straight Talk*.

Jack Fahey, my husband, has been crucial to my staying centered throughout my writing. Thank you for your daily support, feedback, and wonderful discussions emanating from being an "insider."

Again, I thank you all.

Introduction

I have worked in the field of addictive disorders for more than twenty-five years, yet I remain in awe of the strength and courage found in recovering people and their family members. This strength and courage can mend damaged relationships and create healthy, functioning families. It is true that parents feel extremely vulnerable when addressing how their addiction has impacted their children, yet their desire to prevent their children from repeating their own addictive behaviors is both deep and primal.

While this book is written primarily for the recovering addicted parent, it contains information that will be valuable to anyone who has addiction in his or her family system. The "other parent," who may not have an addiction, will certainly find many of the exercises and information relevant. The reader may be a parent who grew up with addiction and realizes his or her child is more at risk than other children. There are few families not affected by addiction in some manner, and all parents can learn from tips on how to talk to their children about alcohol and drugs.

Because addiction to alcohol and drugs is the most notable and predominant of addictions, this type of addiction will be the theme throughout this book. Recognizing that few people are addicted to just a single behavior or substance, I will make reference to other addictions. If your primary addiction is not alcohol or other drugs, you can substitute the name of the appropriate addiction, with the exception of sex addiction. Because of the multitude of ways sex addiction may manifest itself, and the many variables to be considered, I would suggest you share this book with a counselor who specializes in sex addiction and work with him or her about what is and is not appropriate to share with your children.

Addiction dynamics vary greatly in families, so I've tried to represent several scenarios. Perhaps you raised your children in active addiction, not becoming clean or sober until they were of adult age. Perhaps your recovery began midstream in the raising of your children, or you were in recovery prior to ever having children. It is also possible that you have not raised your children at all and have had little contact with them.

Certain sections of this book address issues specific to children of one age group versus another, and of children still under parental supervision or those now living on their own. Overall, each chapter has something for children of all ages.

With those differences in mind, throughout the book I use many people's personal stories to make my points. To illustrate diversity in families, I have depicted five recovering parents, each of whom will be followed throughout this book.

The first parent featured is James, along with his adult children, who had been out of the home for many years when he became sober. Both his children have been drinking since they were teenagers. His son already has two children of his own and is in the process of a divorce.

Dillon is the second parent discussed. His children are now young adults. When they were children, he was preoccupied with his addiction, and, aside from being consistent with child support payments, his relationship with them was that of being a "Disneyland" father. They were left to live with a chronically alcoholic mother who died when they were teenagers. Dillon is so new in his recovery that he hasn't been able to talk with his children about the loss of their mother or what life was like with her.

Next is Kendra. She has one child who has never witnessed the ravages of alcoholism, and a stepchild who has, but who is now exposed to some long-term recovery.

The fourth featured parent is Dina, whose children are still exposed to an angry alcoholic father, even though he is frequently absent from home.

Finally, we will hear of Michael and his children, who have had little exposure to active addiction.

As you come across various scenarios of family situations or examples, simply *take what fits, and leave the rest.*

Let me caution you. You may feel some vulnerability as you read. Because so few addicted people or their spouses claim to have grown up in a healthy, functioning family system, there is a strong likelihood you were raised with addiction and its many losses and hurtful experiences. Some of you may have experienced more blatant trauma, having been subjected to verbal, physical, or sexual abuse. While dysfunction in a family exists on a continuum, usually when addiction presents itself, there has been greater dysfunction within the original family. When that is true it is likely that, as parents, you have had few positive models for healthy parenting. If this is your experience as you are parenting your children, unresolved pain and grief from your childhood are often tapped.

As you read *Straight Talk*, particularly the last two chapters, you may find yourself feeling angry, sad, or depressed. You may think your feelings are inappropriate to the situation described in this book, but you are experiencing the feelings nonetheless. Recognizing that your feelings don't necessarily seem to fit the situation you are reading about is a major cue that you are tapping into old pain.

It will be important to seek a place to talk about the pain of your childhood. This may be in a Twelve Step Al-Anon group, in a codependency group, or with a therapist, a sponsor, your partner, or a close friend. Don't confuse pity with grief. You aren't feeling sorry for yourself; rather, you are feeling the vulnerability of having been hurt many years earlier. Now you have the opportunity to let go of the grief. Many counselors and therapists work with people in recovery while they do family-of-origin work. This will assist you in separating your past pain from present-day parenting skills.

Another vulnerability can occur while reading and working through the information in this book. You need to acknowledge that you may or may not be in agreement with your children's other parent.

A critical factor in healthy parenting depends on the primary parents being cooperative and consistent in their parenting practices. This is difficult enough in traditional families, but in families affected by addiction, the likelihood of blended families and children splitting their time between primary parents is even greater. The unresolved conflict that so frequently remains between ex-partners, and the possibility of one parent still being actively addicted, contributes to even greater inconsistency between parents.

You do what you can to be the best parent you can be. You practice the Serenity Prayer as frequently as needed. You focus your communication on what is best for the children. You practice good boundaries by not saying negative things about their other parent to your children or in front of them. You breathe deeply when your children try to manipulate you with "Well, when I am with Mom (or Dad), she (or he) does it differently. . . ."

In the best of circumstances, parenting is not easy. Parenting requires vigilance. Get support, seek out books about parenting, take a parenting class, see a family counselor if necessary. Take your frustrations and concerns to others you know who have children. You are not alone in parenting! There are many before you and alongside of you. Reach out to them, talk to them.

The Chapters Ahead

Chapter 1, Straight Talk about Addiction and Recovery, focuses on why a parent would choose to talk to a child about addiction to alcohol and drugs. I describe for you the concerns of the five recovering parents previously noted, telling you more about their varying family situations. Motivation and expectations in talking to children will be discussed, and I conclude with ten basic messages that need to be woven into discussion.

Chapter 2, Breaking the Chain of Addiction, helps parents to better understand addiction and its characteristics, such as denial, preoccupation, loss of control, change in tolerance, and withdrawal. The purpose of this is to offer some information in a manner that will allow you to feel more prepared to talk about these dynamics if it is appropriate. Brain chemistry will be discussed. While the focus of the dialogue in this chapter is predominantly oriented toward adolescent or adult-age children, I will conclude the chapter addressing the disease concept with young children.

In this chapter you will be introduced to the Discussion Tips. Throughout the book you will see highlighted sections that will offer you a framework for discussion.

Chapter 3, Generational Vulnerability, addresses genetic and environmental influences that can contribute to becoming addicted to alcohol and drugs. While it may not be relevant to cite the research studies to your child, it will ground you in the facts around addiction and genetics. You will have the opportunity to use several models of discussion for talking about the legacy in your family. I conclude by reminding you about the power of your personal recovery in preventing addiction in your own children.

Chapter 4, Clarifying the Confusion, is written specifically for the recovering parent to have discussions about issues such as multiple addictions, abstinence, slippery places, relapse, and blackouts. You will find several Discussion Tips to lead you toward healthy dialogue. In addition to discussing the aspects of addiction, children need to better understand recovery practices, such as why one attends self-help meetings, why one may choose to do that for many years, and what concerns the family might have around the "religious" aspect of Twelve Step recovery. I will continue to share with you the experiences of our five diverse parents and their families.

Chapter 5, Early Recovery and Making Amends, addresses the issues of guilt, making amends, and self-forgiveness. I talk about the many feelings children have experienced and the delicate nature of beginning to trust and allowing openness.

Chapter 6, New Ways of Relating, uses the featured five parents as examples to illustrate a variety of situations and the different ways each responded to his or her children. I talk about offering validation to your children's experiences and how many parents begin their new relationships simply by *being there*, or in other words, *being present*. I offer reasons why parents decide to talk about the wreckage of their past with their children, and guidelines to follow when it is appropriate. You will find Tips for Listening, and suggestions to support your children in being able to talk with others.

Chapter 7, Creating Healthy Family Traditions, talks about family risk factors that may increase the likelihood of your child abusing alcohol and drugs and protective factors that would decrease such likelihood. This chapter is most helpful to those who are presently raising or will be raising children. The Functioning Family section addresses five pivotal issues: (1) providing support and affirmation; (2) communication; (3) maintaining a positive family identity; (4) problem solving; and (5) providing physical safety. I also encourage those with adult children to look at this section, as several of the Discussion Tips are appropriate for you to explore. Reshaping Family Roles is most helpful if you are currently raising young children, but still important in an informational way to better understand your adult children. Deepening and Mending Relationships will encourage the structure of time with individual family members and the family as a whole. You can be creative with this latter section and discover some wonderful ways to spend time with your adult children too.

Chapter 8, Never Underestimate Your Power as a Parent, speaks to all parents and reinforces the fact that if you have a positive relationship with your children, they do listen to you, and you must offer very direct messages to them about not using alcohol and drugs. I will be very specific about messages to offer children from preschool to adult age.

You cannot make up for the past overnight or in a few conversations; neither can you totally protect your children from the many influences of addiction. As in other areas of your life, this is "a step at a time" process. Some of you will quickly be in step with some children; for others of you, the journey may be slower. This is when it becomes helpful to remember you are not alone. There are thousands of others in recovery with similar experiences and even more parents in general who can offer support and insight. Nearly all parents struggle at times. There is no one prescription for raising children or mending hurt relationships. It is my hope *Straight Talk* will offer you support, guidance, and direction while allowing you to be present for your children with your own authentic style.

Chapter 1

Straight Talk about
Addiction and Recovery

On December 31, 1986, the day after I got sober, the last thing I wanted to face was what I had done to my kids. Prior to sobriety, as a father, what I had going for me was the law, the Ten Commandments, and the tradition that adult men protect their kids. So when I became sober, the first thing I wanted to do was quickly reassert their respect for me based upon everything I had going for me. This might have worked when they were small and I had drank only a short period, but by the time I got sober nobody could say that I deserved all of the respect that the law and the Ten Commandments provided for.

I realized I was going to have to get to know the kids and vice versa. For me it meant being friends first. The kids really wanted me to be a parent, and I wanted to regain their respect. Today I have been in recovery for several years and have regained that respect, but not by asserting what I had in the first place. Instead I earned respect by "letting go" of the outcome of my relationships after I had done all I could to change, trusting that God would then do his thing. — Wally

It has always been my belief that parents truly love their children and genuinely want what is best for them, yet that message often becomes convoluted, inconsistent, and sometimes nearly nonexistent when addiction begins to pervade the family system. As much as parents want to correct this, the focus of early recovery is often on recovery practices, marriage or partnership, and job or career. This is coupled with parents frequently just not knowing what to say to their children or how best to interact with them. This confusion can be as true for the adult child as it is for the adolescent-age or younger child. In many cases it is easy to ignore the issue of what to say or how to interact with your children if someone else, such as an ex-spouse or grandparents, predominantly raises them, or they are adults living on their own. Children can also impede the process by pretending all is just fine in your relationship with them because you are now clean and sober. And, in fact, for many it is better already. Or they may distance themselves from you with aloofness or anger.

The inability to be intimate, to share yourself with your children, to be there for them is one of the most tragic losses in life. Having worked with thousands of addicted parents, I've seen their eyes shimmer with tears and glow with love when they talk about their children. As I wrote this book I interviewed a host of parents, and I was inspired by the depth of love and vulnerability shared as they talked about how their addiction impacted their children, and the hope that their recovery would provide them the positive influence and connection that they would like to have with their children.

What Do You Say to Your Children?

In recovery there is a lot of wreckage of the past that needs to be addressed, and there is a lot of moving forward that will happen as well. What your children want most is to know you love them. They want you to be there for them and with them. That can be difficult to recognize if your children are angry or distant. It can be difficult to do given the priority needed to learn how to live clean and sober. Creating new relationships or mending old relationships doesn't happen overnight. The most important thing you can do for your children is to stay clean and sober. Yet while you are doing that there are so many little steps you can take with your children to begin to be the parent they need and the parent you want to be. It is my hope that this book will help you in this journey. Thomas, a recovering parent, shared this story with me.

My daughter was grown by the time I got sober. More than anything, I loved her and wanted her to know that. I wanted her to know that the parent she saw all of her growing-up years wasn't the real me—that there was this whole other me, this place of love that I had for her that I had lost control of due to my drinking and drugging lifestyle. The hardest part was being honest. Then I had to be willing to listen and not argue with her about how she saw me. I know what she saw. She saw the addict. She couldn't see my place of love; it was too well hidden. So I listened and I didn't need to argue; I was now in my place of love. But I really wanted her to know that the things I had said or done were not the real me. Yet it could sound like a cop-out. I wasn't trying to cop out. She had her experiences because of how I acted in my disease.

I talked; she listened. She talked; I listened. Together we have healed.

Addiction is a devastating disease. It ravages one's physical, mental, emotional, and spiritual being. The greatest pain is that it impacts those we love the most—our children. In recovery we learn that addiction is a disease, that it is not a matter of willpower or self-control. We surrender to our powerlessness over alcohol and other mind-altering chemicals. We put one step in front of the other, often following the direction of other recovering alcoholics and addicts before us. We rejoice and celebrate recovery. For the first time in a long time, we begin to like ourselves. We begin to let go of our insecurities, our fears, and our angers. We begin to look beyond ourselves, and when we do, many of us are confronted with the reality that this disease is not just ours alone. Addiction belongs to the family. Confronted with that stark realization, how do we empower ourselves to make a difference in our children's lives so that they do not repeat our history?

Most children raised with addiction vow to themselves and often to others, "It will never happen to me. I will not drink like my father, or use drugs like my mother." They believe they have the willpower, the self-control, to do it differently than their parents. After all, they have seen the horrors of addiction, and shouldn't that be enough to ensure that they don't become like their parents? If I were to meet with a group of children under the age of nine, raised with addiction, and ask them if they were going to drink or use drugs when they were older, it is very likely that nearly 100 percent of them would vehemently shake their heads no. If I were to come back six years later when these children are teenagers, half of them would already be drinking, using drugs, or both. The majority of the others would begin to drink or use within the next few years.

These children will begin drinking or using out of peer pressure, to be a part of a social group, to have a sense of belonging. Kids often start to experiment just to see what it is like, and many simply like the feeling. Some will find that alcohol and drugs are a wonderful way to medicate or anesthetize the pain of life. Alcohol and drugs momentarily allow their fears, angers, and disappointments to disappear. For some it produces a temporary sense of courage, confidence, and maybe even power. Aside from the emotional attraction that alcohol or drugs may provide, the genetic influence may be such that these children's brain chemistry is triggered within their early drinking or using episodes, and they quickly demonstrate addictive behavior.

As a recovering parent, or spouse/partner, what can you do to stop the chain of addiction? What do you say to your children about your addiction? What you say and do depends on your own story.

Having briefly introduced you to the lives of five recovering parents in the introduction, let's delve more specifically into their different situations.

James is three years sober in his alcoholism. He and his wife are uncertain how to approach their thirty-year-old son and twenty-four-year-old daughter regarding his and her use of drugs and alcohol. James sees so much of himself in his son's behavior when he was that age. He is concerned with his son's simmering anger, his increasing isolation, his daily drinking. Both of his children witnessed the damage of his alcoholism and supported and aligned with their mother during James's heaviest acting out, but up to this point he has never directly discussed his alcoholism. Now that he is sober, he has simply attempted to be a better parent. But there are things he will want to talk about with his adult children. He is also aware that he has the opportunity to be a better role model to his two young grandchildren than he was to his children in their growing-up years. This makes him wonder what his grandchildren should know about addiction. What information would be helpful to them?

Kendra is eleven years clean and sober from her addiction to alcohol and prescription pain pills. She met her husband, Neil, in recovery. Her daughter, now ten years old, was born after Kendra had been sober for one year, so her daughter was never exposed to active addiction. Kendra's stepson witnessed addiction firsthand, as both of his parents were alcoholics. After they divorced he remained with his alcoholic mother until the age of twelve, when he moved in with Kendra and his father. While both children have different experiences in regard to their exposure to addictive behavior, they each have two biological alcoholic parents. Kendra wonders if she and

Neil should talk with and parent the two children differently. She believes much of what she has shared with her daughter about addiction needs to be shared with her stepson. But she and Neil believe they may have very different conversations, as Neil's son has lived with active addiction.

Dina, a practicing member of Al-Anon, lives with her alcoholic husband. They have four children between the ages of six and fourteen. Dina is no longer enabling her husband, as she had for many years, but he is still drinking. He is frequently away from home, but he is surly when he is home and critical of the children. Dina knows she cannot totally protect the children from the hurt of a drunk and often-absent parent, but she is being a much stronger parent and is no longer using them as a buffer between her and her husband and no longer using them as her best friends. While she doesn't want to speak negatively about her husband, she feels her children deserve the truth about their father's alcoholism. She is concerned about whether or not it would be hurtful to tell them he is an alcoholic. She knows her job is to help these children be safe, but she is confused about how to go about that. She also doesn't know how to address the issue of alcohol and drug abuse with her children when their father blatantly abuses alcohol.

Dillon, less than a year sober, has a twenty-three-year-old son and seventeen-year-old daughter. His children lived with their mother until she died four years ago from her alcoholism. He is concerned about his son's drinking and his daughter spending time with kids who have the signs of being drug users. He feels that to start talking to them about their behavior now, just because he is sober, would make him a hypocrite.

Michael is confused about what to say to his eight- and ten-year-old children. He believes they weren't aware of his alcohol and drug addiction and are not aware of his recovery. He always hid his addictive behavior with the excuses of working late hours and sometimes needing to stay overnight at work. His wife was diligent in covering his alibis with the children. He acknowledges that his wife was witness to his out-of-control behavior, as were his co-workers. He was actually put into an impaired physician's program with his license subject to review on an ongoing basis for the first few years of his recovery. While in treatment, the children were simply told that he had to work away from home. Michael has never told them of his addiction or that he regularly attends Twelve Step meetings. His alibis for attending meetings are the same ones he gave for his absences due to his addiction.

Motivation and Expectations

Before you begin a discussion on addiction with your children, it is helpful to clarify your motives and expectations in talking to your children. Here is my rule of thumb:

If your children have lived with addiction, they have the right to understand it. Even if they did not live with addiction, your children deserve to understand addiction for a host of reasons:

- They may be genetically predisposed toward addiction.
- Addiction is a significant part of who you (their parent) are, and talking openly about it allows for the potential of intimacy.
- You can help them to understand your behavior of the past—and your commitment to recovery in the present.
- You can help the child understand how his or her life has been affected.
- Finally, because we live in an addictive culture, they will have others in their lives who will abuse alcohol and drugs.

Take time to examine your motives before talking to your children. Is your motivation the hope that your children will not repeat your behavior? Is it to create a more honest relationship between you and them? Is it to lessen guilt? Is it all of the above and/or more?

While a healthy discussion of addiction is not specifically about making amends, the very fact that you are breaking the Don't Talk Rule begins an amends process. Discussion needs to emanate from healthy thinking and the acceptance of one's own disease and of one's self.

After considering your motivation for talking about your addiction, you also need to think about your expectations to make sure they are realistic. Some children are openly angry. Others may want to take care of you or protect you. "It's all right, don't feel guilty. It wasn't that bad." Others may be polite but indifferent to hearing about addiction or recovery. James's son remarked, "My father wants me to hear about the Twelve Steps when he wasn't even around to tell me about the ABCs. He missed his chance." The purpose of discussing addiction is not for immediate acceptance of the information or of you. It would be my hope that your expectation is that you will be heard. That is a healthy expectation—simply that you will be heard. Your children will take the information, digest it, and make sense out of it for themselves. In the early phase of discussions, kids are more likely to value your behavior in recovery over your words. Children want to see you "walk the walk," not just "talk the talk."

The timing and environment for discussion are very important given that relationships are complex and often have a history fraught with mistrust and a lack of communication. Depending on your relationship, you will be able to reach out more blatantly to some children sooner than others. Adolescent resistance may be strong. In this stage of development children are in the process of individuating and separating psychologically from their parents. They are looking to their peers rather than parents for identification and belonging. In fact, it is natural that they push against their parents as a part of distinguishing their own sense of autonomy, having their own identity. It is possible that a teenager or adult-age child may already be caught up in the web of addiction. Sometimes parents recognize this; other times it is not so apparent.

Remember, discussion is not a onetime event but a process in which conversations occur over time. Opportunities will arise naturally and spontaneously for some discussion, while other conversations will need to be more intentional. The personal experiences shared in this book will offer you direction.

In the enthusiasm of recovery, there may be a degree of impatience with the process. A part of addictive thinking is operating from an all-or-nothing perspective, sharing every thought and feeling or sharing nothing and then acting as if there is but one moment or opportunity to correct the past.

An adult child, in very early recovery, spoke with urgency about needing to fly home immediately to see his mother before she died. He wanted to tell her what he was finding out about himself in sobriety. When asked if she was sick, he replied, "No, she's just getting older." His mother was only forty-seven years old. While his motivation to share was born from enthusiasm and love, his recovery was so new he had not thought out what he wanted to say. Keep in mind that sharing your recovery, like discussing your addiction with your children, is also a process in which conversations occur over time. Be realistic about your expectations and proceed with the intention to have what can be some of the most important conversations of your life.

Time to Act

All of that said, it is vital that you take the opportunity to talk with your children about addiction. You have the opportunity to create change within individual family relationships and within the family as a whole. Recovery begins with breaking what is known as the Don't Talk Rule, or the Rule of Silence. There is no better topic for discussion than to bring up what counselors often refer to as the "elephant in the living room" when referring to addiction.

An important part of this sharing process is reminding children that they are growing up in a society where alcohol and drugs are plentiful. They should be told that they are not alone, that one in four children live in families with alcohol abuse or alcoholism.[1] Countless others have parents who use or abuse drugs. Although abuse of these substances poses a danger to everyone, it is important for your children to know they may carry an especially high risk, and they are four times more likely to develop severe substance abuse problems.[2]

While it is not possible to always prevent alcoholism and drug abuse, exercising caution can make a difference and influence the choices your children make. You can take advantage of the knowledge that alcoholism and drug dependencies run in families and appear to be genetically influenced. Children of addicts are at a greater risk for developing addictive disorders. The more knowledge children have regarding substance abuse and use, and the more children know about the problems that have occurred in their family, the greater their understanding of their own personal risk. Education helps people to make better choices. Research indicates that kids, elementary age and adolescents, do listen to their parents about the important issues in their lives. Their parents' expectations for their behavior are important to kids if they have a positive connection in their relationship.

Regardless of the age of the child, these ten basics need to be woven into discussions about addiction.

1. Children need to hear that you love them, that you always have and always will.
2. Children need to hear you are sorry for your behavior.
3. Children need to know that they are not at fault and in no way did they cause the need for you to drink, use drugs, or engage in any addictive behavior.
4. Children need to know that you would like to have more openness and honesty in the relationship, and that you realize this begins with you.
5. Children need to hear that you will do everything in your power to abstain from the addictive behavior.
6. Children need to know that you will take responsibility for your behaviors and addiction and are now accountable for living differently and being accountable for your recovery.
7. Children need to know that addiction is a family disease, and it often runs through family generations.
8. Children need to know addiction in the family can skip generations.
9. Children need to know that you would like to break the chain of addiction.
10. Children need to know you will listen to their experiences and be available if they want to talk.

What to Say to Your Kids

I love you.

I am sorry.

You are not at fault.

I am responsible for my addiction and now my recovery.

I would like this family to break the chain of addiction, and I believe we can.

Picture yourself teaching your child how to ride a bicycle for the first time. Being a good parent, you choose the right place and time, equip the child with a helmet and appropriate shoes and clothing. The bicycle is the right size, has a bell, and is in overall good condition. You explain how to steer, shift gears, and use the brakes. You give safety instructions and caution the child about potential dangers. In the beginning you walk alongside and hold the child upright. Next you run alongside, still helping to maintain balance. Finally, with great trepidation, you release the bike and the child is riding independently.

This is how you explain and educate your children about addiction in the family. You choose the right place and time to begin the process of sharing. You explain addiction and point out the possibility of genetic predisposition and the risks and dangers of becoming addicted. You tell them you are committed to your recovery, and you will practice it a day at a time. You will guide and protect them and eventually you will let go, and they will be on their own to live their lives independently.

I would like to conclude with this reminder from a recovering parent: "My kids have as much a need for my sobriety as I have for their acceptance."

Chapter 2

Breaking the Chain of Addiction

The mother of my children and I met in treatment. While we had our children in early sobriety, my now ex-wife has resumed her use of alcohol and drugs. So even though our children are young, nine and seven, I am pretty specific with them about addiction. Their mother has primary custody. While it is not a good situation, legally, that is the way it is. My kids tell me about their mother's hidden bottles and about her getting silly when she drinks. They tell me a lot. I have told them that when I was younger I used alcohol and drugs like their mother, but in time I found it did not make me happy. I have told them I used because I was seeking something to make my life different, and I didn't know how to do that on my own. The kids know that both of their parents were at one time in a treatment program. I have explained that sometimes treatment works and other times it does not, but when it doesn't, it usually plants seeds that may make a difference in time. Mostly I believe if I model recovery, then they may have a chance. —Eric

Eric sees his children during weekend visitations, holidays, and the summer months. Eric has little choice but to talk openly and specifically with his children, who are exposed to active addiction. In doing so, he and others in his situation are trying to help their children to separate the addiction from the person. This will help Eric's children understand that their mother's behavior is not meant to be intentionally hurtful to them. Of course the children will still have many feelings, but their ability to make this distinction will help them realize the behavior is not a reflection of their worth or value.

The different choices in what and how much parents share with their children need to be influenced by

- the age of the child
- how much of the active addiction the child witnessed
- the parent's relationship with the child

You will need to find your style and entrances into conversations of what is most meaningful to your children.

While it is important to talk about addiction, be careful to avoid being too wordy, detailed, or intellectual in talking to children of any age. They don't need, nor will they listen to, a lecture. Yet the information is invaluable if presented in a realistic and sincere manner. As I introduce addiction and its characteristics, I'll use scenarios involving the five parents that I've mentioned. These are not sample conversations, but information that is succinct and will hopefully allow you to find your own words to describe or explain your addictive process.

Before you begin a discussion about addiction, it can be helpful to review some basic information to help you answer questions. The next pages will provide you with simple facts about the nature of addiction. Some of you may be very familiar with this information, while others will find the following facts new and very helpful.

Addiction Facts

Alcoholism and drug addictions are diseases. They are diseases that cause changes in the brain, which then drive certain behaviors, characterized by continued use of the drug despite negative consequences. The continued use, in spite of negative consequences, reflects the out-of-control behavior. This doesn't mean that addicts cannot stop using or drinking. Treatment of and recovery from addiction are very possible. Alcoholics and those addicted to other drugs can learn to change their behavior, but doing so is difficult and often requires treatment and major lifestyle changes. This can be compared to heart disease, which may also necessitate major lifestyle changes. We don't blame people for having heart disease. We ask them to follow a certain diet, to exercise, and to comply with medication regimes. So it should be with addiction. We shouldn't blame ourselves for having the disease, but we are responsible for our recovery.

Addiction is the compulsive, continuing use of a mood-altering substance or behavior despite the negative consequences.

Alcohol is the most prevalently abused substance along with nicotine and caffeine. Other substances commonly abused today are cocaine, heroin, prescription pills, marijuana, crystal methamphetamine, and anabolic steroids. There are also behavioral addictions, such as money-related disorders (gambling or spending), eating disorders, sexual addiction, relationship dependency, work addiction, and Internet addiction. No matter what the addiction, a person is engaging in a relationship with a behavior or substance in order to produce a desired mood change, intoxication, or a trance state. People with addictions are often seeking to escape, to garner control or a sense of greater power, or to feel more complete.

While engaged in the behavior or substance, people have a sense of being transformed from feelings of low self-worth to false feelings of great worth and value. The substance or behavior transforms people from feelings of being "less than" to feelings of being "greater than," takes one from a sense of shame to grandiosity, and is often a way of numbing oneself. It can also be the escape or the thrill that comes with addictions such as those that involve great risk like gambling or playing the stock market.

Characteristics of Addiction

All addictions are characterized by

- denial
- preoccupation
- loss of control
- change in tolerance
- withdrawal

Denial

Minimizing, discounting, and *rationalizing* are words for denial. Or as one young daughter of an alcoholic mother said, "Denial is when you pretend things are different than how they really are."

Denial: Pretending things are different than how they really are.

For example, when someone is stopped by a police officer and arrested for driving while under the influence, rather than admit that he or she is guilty of the offense, the person blames the police department for increasing the arrest quota. The person really believes it is the police officer's fault. Similarly, a drug user denies the increased use of cocaine as being significant because the denial is coupled with rationalizing that he or she is entitled to feel good because there is so much stress in his or her life.

Denial preserves the addiction. In other words, the attraction to the substance or behavior supersedes any unsettling thoughts or feelings. Rationalizations and avoiding responsibility fuel what is referred to as a denial system. This ability to minimize, discount, and rationalize is practiced increasingly to the point that denial is a natural response. If someone is not in denial, he or she is faced with overwhelming shame, guilt, powerlessness, fear, and hopelessness. This leads back to denial.

James spent years in denial about his alcoholism. He rationalized he wasn't as bad as his father. His father was a violent alcoholic, while James's behavior was passive. He stayed away from home a lot, didn't show up for the important events in his children's lives, and chronically lied to his wife. Yet he had convinced himself that as long as he wasn't violent like his father, his drinking was okay and he really hadn't hurt anyone. He would say, "So I stayed out late, missed a few events, and wasn't as good to my wife as I could be, but I wasn't a bad man." You can hear the delusional thinking and rationalizing in those very comments.

Preoccupation

Preoccupation means being completely absorbed in thought and action with the process of the addiction. Some examples follow.

A father with an addiction wakes up in the morning thinking about how to acquire his drugs that day. During breaks at work he makes plans for getting the drug, preoccupied with creating excuses for his absence from his child's ball game and experiencing euphoric recall about previous drug use. Euphoric recall, remembering and feeling the payoff that comes with using, actively fuels preoccupation and has been said to "juice" the brain, to titillate the brain to seek the substance.

An alcoholic is anticipating the family reunion she has to attend and the excuses she will need to make up in order to slip away for a drink. A gambler is preoccupied with the losses of the previous night, how he will attempt to hide the losses from his family, and what he will do to make up the losses before anyone is aware. He is totally obsessed with how he could have played differently last night and what he will do to win the next time.

Michael's preoccupation began each morning thinking about his drug stash and anticipating excuses to offer his wife for coming home late. He also found himself thinking about how he was stealing his supply of drugs from the hospital where he worked as a physician and wondering whether or not he had covered his tracks.

Preoccupation may not just be about the anticipation of acquiring the next fix. It can take other forms, such as fixating on the excuses and explanations one might need to hide the addictive behavior. It may also include a chronic focus on feelings of remorse, guilt, or self-loathing.

Preoccupation has many faces. Consider how this woman with an eating disorder sums up preoccupation: "What percentage of the time did I think about food, weight, or body size? Ninety-nine percent of the time."

Loss of Control

Loss of control is the inability to exercise restraint. For example, the alcoholic stops at a bar with the intention of having one or two drinks. Several hours later, having consumed far more than one or two drinks, plus a little cocaine, she heads home. In spite of her best intentions, she is unable to predict and control her usage. In the same manner, a gambler sets himself a limit of $300, win or lose. But caught up in the excitement of the game, and winning up to $1,800, he continues to play until he has lost all his winnings, plus an additional $1,000. A person addicted to food has a similar experience when she successfully limits herself to salad for lunch, but feeling deprived by the salad goes home where no one can see her to eat a half-gallon of ice cream.

Describing her increasing loss of control, Kendra says as a teenager she was using alcohol and marijuana every weekend. She went on to college, and her drinking escalated to using every day. She would talk herself into drinking only on weekends, but the more she attempted to do that, the more she found herself drunk somewhere in the middle of the week. She began to schedule her classes later in the day because she wasn't making it to the morning classes. She broke her leg in a car accident and was prescribed pain pills. That's when she found what she called her "second love." With the loss of control, Kendra began to demonstrate an escalation in her addiction. Soon she was manipulating three different doctors to acquire prescriptions for the daily use of pain pills.

Change in Tolerance

Change in tolerance occurs when the dosage, or level of risk if the addiction is a behavior, escalates in order to achieve the desired effect.

In the past one bowl of ice cream would produce a calming effect for the food addict, but now it takes three bowls. Two drinks used to give the alcoholic a buzz, yet now it takes four or five drinks to feel high. If the addiction involves risk, such as gambling or sex, a change in tolerance implies that the level of risk has escalated.

Dillon seemed content to have one or two drinks in the evening. Gradually he found he needed a third or fourth drink to give him the effect he wanted, and he began making the drinks stronger. He was experiencing a change in tolerance. He believed he was functioning the same even though he was consuming more and more alcohol. As his tolerance escalated, so did his preoccupation with when he was going to get his next drink and with coming up with the excuses to make that happen.

Withdrawal

Withdrawal involves the varying degrees of physical and emotional discomfort the addicted person experiences when he or she abstains from the addictive substance or behavior, typically ranging from days to weeks. Alcohol and drugs have what is known as a half-life, meaning the substance remains in the body long after the use. This half-life varies depending on the substance. As the body is detoxifying, the withdrawal may result in physical discomfort such as agitation, headaches, tremors, paranoia, and dizziness. While the anxiety and depression that can result from withdrawal may be physical, symptoms can also be emotional. While this is evident in substance abusers, emotional withdrawal is also evident in behavioral addictions, such as relationship, sex, or work addiction.

Researchers may find, with further brain chemistry research, that withdrawal from behavioral addictions could be physiologically based as well. No longer engaging in the addictive behavior leaves an incredible void that often creates fear, guilt, and confusion about how to cope with life without the substance or behaviors. These feelings coincide at a time when the addicted person has not yet learned new life skills, creating depression and anxiety masked with irritation and anger.

While alcoholics and addicts already know this, it is important that our kids are told that addiction is not defined by how much, how frequently, or what you drink or use, but by what happens to you when you use alcohol or drugs.

Differences in Usage

Children need to know that substance abusers do not necessarily drink or use daily. Many will be binge drinkers or users. They are able to not use or drink daily, and they may maintain control for days or even weeks and months. But when they do drink or use, they usually do so to excess, and it has consistently negative consequences to them and often to others.

What is also confusing to kids is that some people move through the progression of their addiction more quickly than others. For example, if someone is addicted to alcohol, it can take several years before this person moves to late stages of addiction. Yet a cocaine user can move to the late stages of addiction much quicker.

A genetic predisposition can cause a person to move through the progression more quickly. For example, James said he never had a day of normal drinking. From the day he started drinking, alcohol was central to his life. He quickly began experiencing preoccupation and loss of control. He also quickly went into rationalizations and denial about the seriousness of his drinking. This progression can occur more frequently when one has a family history similar to James's. Both of his grandfathers, his father, aunts and uncles on both sides of the family, and his only brother are all alcoholic.

On the other hand, Dillon tells us that his drinking had the appearances of being more normal, occasional, and nonproblematic the first several years he drank. His addiction was more insidious, creeping up on him slowly and inconspicuously.

Another variable that influences the rate of progression is the choice of drugs. Some drugs, such as heroin, cocaine, and methamphetamine, are more quickly addictive than others. The most important point here is that people do progress through their addiction at different paces. It does not make them less addicted.

Seldom is a person addicted solely to alcohol. Alcoholics frequently have co-occurring addictions, meaning substance disorders and behavioral addictions coexist. Women in particular are often addicted to prescription pills and alcohol. A high percentage of gamblers and people with eating disorders are alcoholic. Sex addicts are frequently cocaine addicts. All addicted people, whether they have behavioral or substance addictions, engage in the characteristics of denial, preoccupation, loss of control, change in intolerance, and withdrawal.

Because alcohol is the most pervasive intruder in the life of an addict, it is more common to discuss the alcoholic, but the following example can be useful to describe how a behavioral addiction is similar to a substance addiction.

Like a latter-stage drug addict or alcoholic, compulsive gamblers live from fix to fix, throwing life away for another roll of the dice and deluding themselves that luck will soon smile on them. Their subjective cravings can be as intense as those of drug abusers. They show tolerance through increased betting, and they experience highs rivaling that of a drug. Up to half of all pathological gamblers show withdrawal symptoms that mimic a mild form of drug withdrawal, including churning stomach, sleep disturbance, sweating, irritability, and craving.[1] And like drug addicts, they are at risk of sudden relapse even after many years of abstinence. This analogy applies to other behavioral addictions as well.

Another complicating factor in addiction is that, contrary to men, it is not uncommon for women who have not abused alcohol in their early adult years to become addicted during midlife. One can postulate a variety of scenarios, but some women use the external control of household busyness to contain the amount or frequency of their alcohol or other drug consumption. With the absence of this control, their use and abuse become more apparent. Also, women's addiction, more than men's, is often precipitated by a loss in life, such as the last child leaving home, divorce, or a death in the family. These losses may be common but are significant triggers for women and addiction.

Females also move through the progression of their addiction more quickly than men, developing a more rapid dependence. When this occurs, it may be very confusing for children who are mid to late teenagers or living out of the home. They didn't see the use of alcohol and have difficulty thinking of their mother as alcoholic or addicted. When children are older and more focused on their own lives, mothers can more easily hide their use of alcohol or drugs. As well, many women's drug of choice is prescription pain pills, and the use of pills is not as obvious as the use of alcohol or other drugs.

Combining a woman's ability to hide the addiction with the stigma of being an addicted woman makes it easier for children to discount their mother's alcoholism or addiction. Kids often minimize or blatantly deny that their mother is "really" an alcoholic. With mothers more so than fathers, children want to say, "It wasn't really that bad."

Brain Chemistry

There is no doubt in my mind that your children are more interested in whether or not you will stay clean and sober and what will happen in their relationship with you than they are in understanding the neurochemistry of addiction. But understanding a few basics of what we know about brain chemistry may at some point be helpful in a discussion.

Today scientists are able to clearly recognize how changes in brain activity are significant in addiction, and they believe that the problem of addiction is centered in the brain.

Scientists have traditionally confined their use of the term *addiction* to substances, namely alcohol and other drugs that clearly foster physical dependence in the user. That is now changing as new knowledge about the brain's reward system and the advancement of technology to study brain images suggest that as far as the brain is concerned, any reward is still a reward, regardless of whether it comes from a chemical or an experience. In other words, what is going on inside the head of a person with one addiction is similar to what goes on inside the head of someone with a completely different addiction. Where there is a reward, there is a risk of the vulnerable brain getting trapped in a repetitive cycle that fuels addiction.[2]

> **Where there is a reward, there is a risk of the vulnerable brain getting trapped in a repetitive cycle that fuels addiction.**

In the brain, substances or repetitious behaviors produce a marked increase of a chemical called dopamine. This creates a change in the brain's experience of pleasure and reward. Increased dopamine stimulates the "reward pathways," which offer vivid, positive feelings and memories of the experience by the release of the neurotransmitter dopamine. While individual drugs work slightly differently on the brain, each triggers the release of dopamine or enhances its "feel-good" effects. These actions create and reinforce the compulsion to take the drug or repeat the behavior.[3]

It is possible that people with addictions have compromised their natural pleasure reward systems in long-lasting ways. Chronic use of a drug to stimulate certain neurotransmitters may reduce the brain's natural ability to produce the neurotransmitters without the drug. People who are addicted initially take the drug because it makes them feel good. But over time they take it just to feel normal. The addict is then striving just to feel stable, not necessarily high, but the effort becomes futile.

The effect of this "stimulant-reward system," as researchers call it, explains the great appeal of drugs and alcohol. But why do people continue to crave a substance that they may no longer enjoy or that they know is hurting them and those they love? The answer is that all of these substances actually change the way the brain functions.

The brain adapts to the constant input of drugs or alcohol and relies on greater quantities to achieve the same effect. Once the brain becomes less sensitive to dopamine, it becomes less sensitive to natural "reinforcers," such as the pleasure of seeing a friend or watching a movie. The only stimuli still strong enough to activate the sputtering motivation circuit are drugs. In essence, it is possible for someone's motivational priorities to be "rearranged" via brain circuitry.

Memory research is also suggesting a type of nonconscious memory, called sensitization, which may alter neural circuitry involved in normal processes of incentive, motivation, and reward. It is suggested that sensitization in an environment where presumably a person has learned to expect a drug renders brain circuitry hypersensitive to drugs and drug-associated paraphernalia.

Also, brain neurons, which are dulled by the overabundance of certain chemicals, compensate by becoming more easily excitable. The disappearance of the substances causes many of the painful physical symptoms of withdrawal. When the addicted person abstains from the use of the abused substance, he or she may become depressed and anxious, and experience intense cravings for the drug.[4]

In addition to helping us to understand that the center of addiction resides in the brain, this research is helping us to understand that while the "drug of choice" may be different, the behaviors associated with addiction are similar.

Kids and the Disease Concept

Three nine-year-old boys are standing in a long line at Disneyland, waiting to get on one of their favorite rides. In conversation, one boy asks of the other, "When is your dad getting out of the hospital?" Before the boy whose father is in the hospital has a chance to answer, the other boy says, "I didn't know your dad was in the hospital, what happened to him?" The third boy responds, "Oh, he is sick. He has a disease; it's called *al-co-hol-ism.*"

Younger children more readily accept that their parent has a disease; it makes sense to them. This boy's response was reflected spontaneously, without embarrassment, totally accepting that his father genuinely has a disease. Why else would someone act like this? Children prior to the age of nine or ten don't need a lot of explanation. They accept that addiction is a disease with both physical and psychological ramifications. Of course those aren't the words used, but they understand the "being stuck" aspect of addiction, or the allergy analogy. They comprehend that this isn't just a disease that affects someone physically like most diseases. They see the change in personality, and they grasp the inability to stop something once it is started.

A good rule of thumb: When talking to young children, keep explanations to three or four sentences. Let them come back to you with questions.

Many years ago I wrote a book for children affected by parental substance abuse titled *My Dad Loves Me, My Dad Has a Disease.* The title came from the impact of a conversation I had with Alexis, an eight-year-old girl, whose father was alcoholic and in treatment. I was having an individual session with her, and I asked her if she knew why her father was in the hospital. She looked at me as if I was stupid and quickly said, "Of course, he has a disease."

This young girl was able to accept that there was no other reason for her father's behavior. He certainly wouldn't choose to act like he does. Something had happened to him, and he needed help to get well. She had been told that drinking made him sick, that it does that to some people, that it can change his personality so that he behaves in ways that are confusing, scary, and hurtful to him and others. She readily accepted that. Still looking at me as if she wondered what assistance I could be to her since I didn't seem to know her father had a disease, she added, "But he still loves me." Alexis fully believed this because in her case her father had provided positive parenting in her very early years, and she got the message that he loved her.

It is possible to talk to a child of any age as long as age-appropriate language and relevance are considered. With young children this conversation is likely to be more brief and much more general. Parents often tell them that they are allergic to alcohol and when they drank they did things they wish they didn't do. So now they choose not to drink. If children are aware of your drug use, you can tell them that you made some poor choices and used drugs and then couldn't stop on your own, or without help. Again, if they have lived with it, or saw you many times when you were under the influence, it is best to acknowledge it.

I have worked with children as young as four and five years of age who can describe personality changes and even loss of control, though they don't use that language. Some poignant explanations of personality change and loss of control I have heard from young children have been, "Sometimes my mom is very loving toward me and really likes me, and then maybe later in the day she acts like a stranger to me." "When my dad says he is going to the bar for one or two drinks, he just can't do that anymore. It is sort of like eating potato chips; I eat the whole bag." As adults we often underestimate how much children have witnessed and understood.

Other parents find that if their children did not witness the active addiction and only know their parents in recovery, it is best to be less specific about the addiction until the children are older and it has more relevance to each child's life.

> *I have always been vague with my kids about just what I took, how much or how frequently I drank—but they know I drank a lot and chose to stop when we had our first son. I see them as boys who could idealize the partying way of life, and if it was good enough for their dad and he ultimately stopped, then they could rationalize it is okay for them and that they could stop. I can remember one night when I was really loaded, sitting in a pickup truck with friends, smoking a joint when a friend's thirteen-year-old son came up to the truck. This was a kid who idolized me. I can remember him just staring at me with this strange look on his face. That boy never related to me again. I don't want my boys to ever see me as that boy did. —Kevin*

As children raised with addiction become older they are not so readily willing to accept the disease model as the answer for why or how you, their parent, behaved the way you did. If children have not had some formal education about addiction, they may very well think calling it a disease is a cop-out. They may think you are trying to make excuses for your behavior and blame it on something other than yourself. If you are met with that resistance, your job is not to convince them; your job is simply to share information.

You'll find children may listen more if you do the following things:

- Be descriptive about the addiction.
- Take ownership for your choices along the way and how you were ignorant about what you were doing. Explain that you didn't realize you could not stop and pretty soon you were rationalizing, denying, etc.
- Identify how horrific the consequences were becoming.
- Relate that you needed help to stop something that had become bigger than you.
- Be more available to them now that you are in recovery.

You don't have to convince your children of anything or convert them to your way of thinking; just share yourself with them.

Tell your children the areas of your life in which you believe you were out of control, such as using alcohol or drugs, spending and debting, or working.

Refer to how your addiction controlled your life by speaking of your preoccupation and denial. Give your children examples of the extent of your denial and rationalization. Tell them this is not what you envisioned when you started your addictive behaviors, and that you had no idea how it was hurting the family in spite of what were obvious signs.

Describe your change in tolerance and/or escalation to achieve the desired effect.

Make the point that you continued your behavior in spite of adverse consequences—again demonstrating that your addiction had power over and against your good judgment and morality.

You do not need to cover every point in only one conversation. This is not necessarily the only conversation you will have; hopefully it may be a part of many conversations.

Perhaps you and your children are watching a movie and you identify with one of the characters in the movie. In the car, on the way home, while the kids are talking about the movie, you can offer how you recognized yourself. For example, you may say, "When that teenage girl thought no one knew what she was doing, when she was stealing her mother's things, that was a lot like me when I was drinking and using. I thought I was being so sneaky, but by the time I quit nearly everyone knew I had a problem. I kept rationalizing, just like she did in the movie."

What is paramount in these conversations is that children hear that they did not cause the addiction, and they can't control it.

Chapter 3

Generational Vulnerability

What I remember about my childhood is that my father and his father were alcoholics. When I started coming home loaded and getting into trouble, nobody acted like anything was wrong. They didn't do anything to stop my behavior. I lived with a drunken parent. My dad lived with a drunken parent. The difference is my kids don't see me drunk. They won't ever have the visual and mental impact that I had and my father had. For my kids, alcoholic behavior won't be their norm. I am breaking the link. —Mark

Knowledge by itself is not going to be enough to stop your children from using drugs or drinking alcohol, or from becoming addicted. But it is an important aspect to healthy parenting and a significant part of the parenting package in discussing alcohol and drugs.

If addiction has been a part of your family history, it is important for you to share that information with your adolescent and adult-age children. It is possible, and quite likely, that there has been a family member who has not self-identified an addiction, or other family members have not called it addiction. However, you can name it or indicate that you think the behavior is addictive.

For example, you might say, "My grandfather was never referred to as an alcoholic, but his behavior certainly indicated that he had a problem with alcohol." Then give examples of the behavior. Use this as an opportunity to talk about the many different types of addictions that frequently permeate a family. For example, you might say, "My drug of choice was cocaine, but my mother was addicted to prescription pills and her father was an alcoholic." Or, "My mother and I both have eating disorders, and my father and his father were alcoholics."

33

Family Tree

The following is a picture of the history of addiction in two extended families. Each family tree reflects how addiction has permeated several generations. It is often difficult to have family information past one's grandparents, but if you do, go as far back in the family history as you can. Whether or not you choose to take the opportunity to explore this, just giving thought to your family tree will be helpful in discussing genetic predisposition and how environment influences the vulnerability for addiction.

To do a family tree, please refer to appendix 1 at the back of the book for a form that will assist you. Or, make your own diagram allowing for the span of several generations. This can be a meaningful family exercise in which all members have input. It offers a good opportunity to talk about family history.

Begin with grandparents on both sides of your family. Then note any siblings for both of your parents and their children. You may note them by name, if you have names, or refer to them as a boy or girl. Then note the person whose tree it is, their brothers and sisters, and any children. Include any deceased relatives as well. You can look at many aspects of your family, but for the purpose of this book, begin by looking at addictions. Begin by circling any names of people you suspect had addictive disorders. You can also use symbols or colors. You may want to begin with those who had alcohol or drug problems. Depending on the age of your children, decide whether you want to include other addictions and issues such as family abuse.

James, who is concerned about passing down the legacy of addiction to his two children, clearly has a history of addiction for the past three generations. Both grandfathers and his father were alcoholics. James has one aunt on his father's side of the family and two uncles on his mother's side of the family who were addicted. His brother has a problem with compulsive sex and cocaine, and his sister has been married to two addicted men. Now his sister's teenage daughter is using.

Dina, who is presently married to an alcoholic, discovered when she completed her family tree that she also had two alcoholic grandfathers. Neither of her parents was alcoholic, but both of her brothers are and she married an alcoholic. In Dina's case addiction actually appears to have skipped a generation.

James's Family Tree

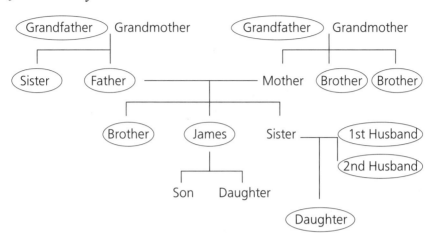

Dina's Family Tree

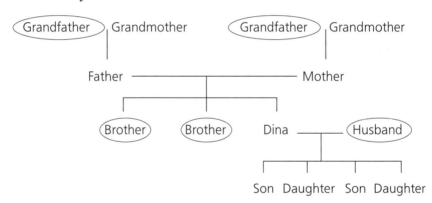

Genetic Influences: The Facts

Strong scientific evidence suggests that alcoholism tends to run in families.

FACT: Children of alcoholics are more at risk for alcoholism and other drug abuse than children of nonalcoholics.[1]
It is estimated that 13 to 25 percent of children of alcoholics will become addicted. There is no identifiable person more likely to become alcoholic than this child. This is an extremely high percentage compared to children in nonalcoholic homes.

FACT: Alcoholics are more likely than nonalcoholics to have an alcoholic father, mother, sibling, or other relative.[2]
Research indicates that almost one-third of any sampling of alcoholics has at least one parent who is or was an alcoholic. Treatment programs are more apt to say minimally 50 percent or more of addicted clients are children of alcoholics. This does not mean that 50 percent of children of alcoholics become addicted. It means that, more likely than not, those who become addicted are the biological children of an alcoholic.

FACT: Alcoholism has a strong genetic predisposition.[3]
Sons of alcoholic fathers are at a fourfold risk of becoming addicted compared with the sons of nonalcoholic fathers. To date the research has been predominantly conducted on sons living with fathers who are alcoholic. However, duplicate studies of children adopted close to birth offer convincing evidence of an increased risk for severe alcohol problems, even when the child had no knowledge that his biological parent had alcoholism.

There are many studies that support a genetic theory of alcoholism transmission. The works of Marc Schuckit, M.D., and Henri Begleiter, Ph.D., have been pivotal in the growing understanding of the genetic predisposition.

Marc Schuckit conducted a notable, long-term study of sons of alcoholics. In his twenty-year study, he found males with a family history of alcoholism appear to have a lower intensity reaction to alcohol's effects than those without this type of family history. They are not experiencing an awareness of the effects of alcohol as early as others would be aware of being under the influence. This means that while one young man feels tipsy at two drinks, the child with the biological alcoholic father not only doesn't feel tipsy, he also feels only slightly more relaxed than before he drank the alcohol. This low level of response to alcohol has been shown to be characteristic of sons of alcoholics and to predict alcoholism almost a decade later.[4]

Son of nonalcoholic	Son of alcoholic
2 drinks = tipsy	2 drinks = nontipsy
experiences negative response earlier	takes much longer to experience negative effect

Here is a more simple way to talk about Schuckit's research. Jesse's mom is alcoholic. Jesse's best friend, Heather, lives across the street and her mom is not an alcoholic. Jesse's mother exhibited some embarrassing behavior while the young girls were playing together. Jesse and Heather made a pact that they would never drink because they didn't want to be like Jesse's mother when she drank. Later, when they were in eighth grade, Jesse and Heather were visiting some boys down the street. The boys offered them a wine cooler. Heather took the wine cooler. Jesse confronted Heather, "What are you doing? We agreed we would never drink." Heather said, "Oh, come on, one won't hurt." Heather was giddy after one wine cooler, but Jesse did not feel any effect. Jesse noticed how much fun Heather was having so she drank a couple more coolers in order to feel what Heather was feeling. Jesse is now learning the mood swing that is associated with alcohol use, and she is experiencing a greater tolerance for alcohol than her friend Heather.

Henri Begleiter was the first to characterize brain dysfunction in alcoholics and is known for conducting the breakthrough research that showed genes are involved in the development of alcoholism. He discovered neurophysiological deficits in some brain systems of abstinent chronic alcoholics. His studies indicated that with long-term abstinence, many of the harmful effects of alcohol on the brain improved substantially, while a few irregularities did not recover with prolonged abstinence.

Most significantly, Begleiter and his co-workers would continue to discover that such neurophysiological anomalies were present in the offspring of alcoholics who had never been exposed to alcohol or other drugs. The brain anomalies reflect hyperexcitability that is temporarily alleviated by the ingestion of alcohol. It is this hyperexcitability that is inheritable and thus increases one's risk for alcoholism.[5]

Overall, the results of many biological studies indicate that children of alcoholics react differently to alcohol or other drugs because of a difference in biochemical transmission. In summary, research suggests the following points:

- Children of alcoholics may suffer chemical imbalances that make them prone to substance-abusing behaviors.
- Children of alcoholics have increased feelings of pleasure and

relaxation from alcohol ingestion, increased elation and/or decreased muscle tension in response to alcohol ingestion, decreased feelings of intoxication at the same blood alcohol levels compared with children of nonalcoholics, and a possible serotonergic deficiency or an exaggerated level of serotonin when ingesting alcohol.

Genetic researchers are adamant that we understand that it is not alcoholism that is inherited; it is the biological vulnerability to the disease that is inherited.

This does not mean that if children of alcoholics drink they will become alcoholic; it means the brain chemistry is such that there is a far greater likelihood due to the vulnerability. It is estimated that genetics account for approximately 40 to 60 percent of the risk of the development of alcohol abuse or dependence.[6]

Addiction can so easily begin in innocence, but as it says in the Big Book of Alcoholics Anonymous, "Remember that we deal with alcohol—cunning, baffling, powerful!"[7]

Environmental Influences: What's in the Psychology?

While it is common for children who recognize they are being raised with chemical dependency to say they will not drink or use when they get older, in reality most choose to do so. They begin to drink and use at about the same ages and for similar reasons as children of nonaddicted families. But most significantly, if raised with addiction in the family, they drink or use with an added belief that *it will never happen to me*. This is a belief that ascribes to knowing that their parent is chemically dependent but believing that addiction is a lack of willpower, that it is a control issue. This belief says, "I have seen enough and I know enough about what alcohol or drugs can do to a person. I will be different."

For children who have grown up with addiction of any type, it often means they grew up with confusion, fear, shame, loneliness, and powerlessness. The substances or the behavior they would come to abuse often provided relief, something they did not know how to seek naturally. For example, alcohol may give a sense of power to someone who has only known powerlessness. It may give access to feelings of courage and confidence to someone who feels inadequate. This false empowerment is certainly drug-induced and temporary, but for many people a false form is perceived as better than none.

For someone who is isolated and feels alienated from others, being under the influence of alcohol or other drugs may make it easier to reach out to people. This kind of thinking doesn't mean that a person is addicted, but it does mean he or she is thirsty for a connection with others. In this case alcohol becomes the social lubricant in order to feel whole and complete.

Although many of the same personality shifts occur in most people who drink, for those who have a history of pain, substances may be the only things they find to provide relief. Taking a drink or using drugs may make them feel adequate—a feeling that to be sustained leads from one drink or snort to another. When these individuals are using, they are able to become open with their feelings. They may show some vulnerability and discover that other people respond to them more positively when they exhibit this relaxed and open manner. This does not necessarily make them chemically dependent, but it does reinforce their need to drink or use, and it sets them up for a psychological dependency and a higher level of vulnerability to addictive use.

Some people may find themselves aware of previously undiscovered options and alternatives. Making decisions becomes easier. In order to maintain these feelings and behaviors it seems reasonable to rationalize taking another drink, using drugs, or acting out the addictive behavior. There comes a time when life can't be experienced without the use or abuse of the primary drug of choice. Again, there is a setup for a dependency.

The discovery that alcoholism is influenced by genetic factors does not mean that genes alone cause severe alcohol problems. It is more likely to be the inherited vulnerability (genetics) coupled with psychological injury. Environmental factors do play a role.

For those who become more focused on others, to the exclusion of any self-focus, drinking or using may help them talk more freely about themselves; it helps them to feel more self-worth. The drug may contribute to becoming more assertive, to feeling a greater selfishness. It may even help to garner anger, which the anger-avoidant person may find empowering. If being under the influence of alcohol provides feelings of increased self-worth, or an avenue to becoming more assertive, it is natural that someone would respond positively to these new feelings and behaviors. In fact, that person would find he or she needs that support to bolster these feelings. Drinking or using then becomes the problem solver. Before long the psychological trap of substance dependency becomes a reality.

Alcohol and drugs are typical trademarks of rebellious acts for many problematic children. Substances provide an avenue that allows them to feel better about themselves and offers them a false sense of confidence in their abilities. While most acting-out children experiment with alcohol, some quickly become abusers and develop their chemical dependency at earlier ages than other children from addictive families.

 What did alcohol, or your drug of choice, do for you? It can be very helpful for your child to know the role it played in your life.

Did alcohol or drugs give you a feeling of power?

Did it help you feel complete?

Did it deaden emotional pain?

Did it take you out of the feelings of despair and depression?

What did you believe you couldn't do or be unless you engaged in your addictive behavior or substance?

Had you ever said to yourself, "It will never happen to me"?

What do you believe you can do or be today in recovery?

While the previous examples reflect the use of alcohol or other drugs that fuel an addiction, often the legacy is passed down through a different addiction. Other addictions may include food, work, money disorders, or sex. Many of the substances or behaviors to which people become addicted are socially sanctioned and supported, making it very difficult for abusers to see how they are using them in unhealthy ways.

Reanna vowed she would not be like her mother, who is addicted to prescription pills, but found herself with a major spending and gambling disorder. Her relationship with money was just like her mother's relationship with pills. Money was her escape. It gave her false confidence and esteem. Reanna, who always felt powerless, felt power with money. But it was never enough. There was always a hole inside of herself that she was trying to fill.

Casey grew up with a father who was a loud, boisterous, angry alcoholic and sex addict. His dad was flagrant in his sexual acting out and was known as the town womanizer. While Casey did not become a substance abuser, nor was he as flagrant in his sexual acting out as his dad, he did repeat the sexual addiction. His addiction manifested itself predominantly through pornography on the Internet.

Shawna, raised with two alcoholic parents, found solace and answers to her pain in her addiction to food. She said, "Food was love and attention. I would sit and eat ice cream out of the container with my dad. It was a way to connect with him. My mom, who tried to control everything about me, would get angry with me because of my binging. Food was my way of breaking away from her and rebelling. It was the solution to my pain. It became my friend. In my relationship with food I learned how to rebel, be sneaky and dishonest. My behavior was not a whole lot different than theirs as alcoholics."

If there was addiction in your family and your addiction is different from the one you grew up with, share what it is and how it served the same purpose as the drug or behavior you grew up with. This is very important, as children who have an addicted parent are very confident that they will not repeat the patterns of their parent. They delude themselves, frequently finding solace, refuge, and power in a different drug of choice.

After this discussion, take time to go back to your family tree and include other addictions that you didn't recognize before.

The beauty of recovery is that you are now in a position to do what you could not do previously—be a healthy parent. Not perfect, just healthy, at least healthier than before. Recovery is a process. Never forget that your recovery alone demonstrates two very powerful statements to your children of any age: It is okay to ask for help, and people can change. Your recovery models this for them; it is nonarguable.

Chapter 4

Clarifying the Confusion

When I went to treatment for my eating disorder I was confronted with how my use of alcohol and drugs was intertwined. My two teenage daughters were very shocked when they attended family week and heard me say I was an alcoholic and an addict. When I explained to them how my addictions operated as a package, they then understood more about my relapses. I was not able to stay in recovery from my eating disorder until I was abstinent from alcohol and drugs. My family is pretty tired of my relapses and my multiple treatments, but this makes sense to all of us. It will be easier for them to support my recovery now that we all understand my addictions better. —Pam

In the previous chapter I gave you a framework for talking about addiction and the family legacy, but it is often the "here and now" of what you are doing that needs even more discussion. Many aspects of addiction and recovery are confusing, such as multiple addictions, total abstinence, relapse, and certain recovery practices. The following material will offer you some ideas on how to discuss such areas.

Claiming Multiple Addictions

It may be confusing for children when a parent begins recovery or enters a treatment program for one addiction, and soon begins to identify multiple addictions. For example, one father's primary addiction is cocaine, and his drinking doesn't appear to be problematic in and of itself. The children didn't see Dad drinking excessively; they didn't experience the wreckage that is often associated with alcoholism. But they certainly lived with the damage of his cocaine use. So why does Dad now say he is also alcoholic? This is called addiction interaction disorder, which is when one or more addictive substances or processes relate to each other in a manner that re-inforces one or both addictive behaviors. In this case Dad always begins with a few drinks prior to using cocaine. Alcohol, for him, is a disinhibitor. He then uses alcohol to relax when he crashes from the high of the cocaine. The two drugs operate as a package with each other.

The First Step of Alcoholics Anonymous, "We admitted we were power-less over alcohol—that our lives had become unmanageable," is accurate here. While Dad only used alcohol as a disinhibitor for his use of cocaine, he could not stop drinking even though he was fully aware of the conse-quences. He was powerless and his life was unmanageable.

Think of addiction as a car. To get the car started you have to use the ig-nition. In this last example alcohol is the ignition and cocaine is the fuel.

Another example of addiction interaction disorder occurs when one ad-diction is used to cover up the other. A high percentage of gamblers are also known to be alcoholic. While alcohol is the most visible problem and ap-pears to have created the wreckage of their past, the gambling goes un-recognized as a primary addiction. The person uses alcohol to mask the gambling problem by saying, "I gamble because I drink. If I didn't drink I wouldn't gamble." Whether or not this is true, this addict has to give up both drinking and gambling because they operate as a package.

Still another form of addiction interaction disorder occurs when one ad-diction replaces another over time. Someone recovers from alcoholism only to find him- or herself with an eating disorder or a work addiction that shows up several months or a couple of years later.

Another possibility is that the second addiction has always been there but went unrecognized because the first addiction was more noticeable. It is also possible the second addiction manifests after some recovery from the first has occurred. This typically occurs because the psychological need for the drug remains. Think of an onion and its many layers. Peel off the outer layer and you find a second and a third layer—but it is all the same onion. Different addictive behaviors or substances are used to provide what-ever the original addiction psychologically provided, whether it provided a sense of medication, relaxation, power, or control.

Cross-tolerance occurs when one addiction replaces another with little time between them. For example, an alcoholic who stops drinking may become addicted to tranquilizers or pain pills within a year of recovery. Physicians who specialize in addiction treatment often refer to Valium and Librium as "dry martinis."

Multiple addictions can be thought of as two or more addictions operating at the same time, like a wagon being pulled by a team of horses. Sometimes one horse pulls the wagon, representing a single addiction, but it could be two, three, or even four horses.

If you have multiple addictive behaviors, share with your children how you have used the substances or behaviors as a package and how they interact.

Some children will readily accept the concept of multiple addictions, as it makes sense to them. Children who appear to be confused are most likely still angry about the disruption the addiction has caused in their lives and don't want to hear about the complexity of multiple addictions. Your job is not to convince them but to share honestly and openly.

Abstinence

Addictions like alcoholism, drug addiction, and gambling have a more definitive picture of what it means to be abstinent. Recovery from these addictions is typically defined by abstinence from certain types of behaviors. Understanding your need for total abstinence on a continuous basis is significant for family members. If they have a difficult time grasping the idea of total abstinence—that you can never engage in your addictive behavior again, not even a little—share with them how that information impacted you when you first became aware that abstinence is the most common recommendation for recovery.

Most alcoholics and addicts, when confronted with that information, don't just respond with curiosity, as a family member might. Instead they react with internal despair, for abstinence seems unrealistic and impossible. Ultimately, learning to practice recovery one day at a time allows any fears of "forever" to dissipate.

Kendra's stepson was very surprised to learn his stepmother had eleven years of sobriety. "Does this mean you have not had any alcohol in eleven years, not even one drink? And you won't ever drink again?" he asked. Kendra explained to him that total abstinence was a choice she made in order to realize the gifts of recovery.

She also said she makes no promises for the future. By addressing her recovery a day at a time she has no difficulty saying, "Today, I choose to live an alcohol- and drug-free life." She also added, "If I drink again, I have to be willing to pay the penalty and impose the consequences on myself and my family. I cannot safely drink. Once I have a mind-changing chemical in my system, my defenses are down. I can no longer trust myself to think honestly and I begin to rationalize, minimize, and deny." The addicted person cannot *safely* drink or use again. Safely means without grave risk.

Talk with your children about your thoughts on abstinence and what tools you use to deal with the "forever" issue, such as living a day at a time.

Slippery Places

In early recovery addicted people are strongly advised to stay away from "slippery places." Such triggers are locations and people who remind the recovering person of situations where he or she once practiced the addiction. The external triggers are too available and the pressures of such an environment are often too strong for the recovering person. For example, an alcoholic would stay away from bars. The smells, the music, seeing the multitude of bottles on the back shelf, and being surrounded by drinking buddies are all strong triggers.

James knew he had to give up baseball games—for him the drinking there was more important than the game. Sometimes recreational activities become pastimes in which drinking or using is central to the experience. In these circumstances the recovering person will choose not to set up situations in which to be triggered and will avoid such activities for a period of time.

If your children have responded to previous talks about brain chemistry, they might also be interested to know that memory researchers recognize that an addict's brain responds to cues in the absence of conscious awareness.

Memory researchers divide memories into those you consciously remember and those you don't remember. Consciously, someone may remember a past drug-induced euphoria and seek out the drug again, or one may remember that drugs stopped him or her from feeling crummy. This type of memory explains why people take drugs, but it doesn't explain addiction. Plenty of people drink and use drugs for pleasure-related reasons, but addiction is different. Despite a strong will to quit, once addicted, people compulsively drink or seek out and take drugs, even if it no longer provides pleasure.

Nonconscious memories are much more insidious and more likely to underlie the compulsive aspect of addiction and the cravings that lead to relapse. For instance, the paraphernalia of drug use or the sound of ice tinkling in a glass can act as triggers that induce cravings in the addict, much like the sound of the bell that caused Pavlov's dogs to salivate. It is like hearing the ice cream truck coming down the street when you are a child. Even though addicts can become conscious of the relationship between some drug-related triggers and their cravings, other triggers might be less obvious. For instance, they might not recognize that a certain place or smell awakens in them a hunger for the drug. In the absence of conscious awareness, triggers can goad an individual to seek out the drug of choice.[1]

Memory research supports a stronger argument for involvement in a group recovery process where one is being as honest as possible, listening to others, seeking feedback, and following direction.

Let your children know that abstinence is not as great a loss to you as they may think it is, but, in fact, it is a gain. It has offered you the opportunity to change, to grow, to be the person you want to be. Let them know that recovery is creating new ways of relaxation, connection with others, and an enjoyable life. You can explain to them that if you need to go into a place or engage with someone who you consider a trigger, you will have a valid reason for doing so and will take specific precautions. Let your children know you are responsible for taking care of you. Let them know of your level of comfort in the various settings in which you and they typically spend time together. It is possible that you will need to find different places in which to spend time with your children. Talk with them about where these places might be and problem solve any concerns your children may express.

Relapse

To not discuss relapse is to stay in denial about the possibility of it. It is very likely that prior to an ongoing recovery you attempted to stop the addictive behavior, may have garnered some sobriety, and then relapsed. Family members have seen this happen and are very aware it could happen again.

When someone has had some sobriety from an addiction, if that person re-engages in the addictive behavior, he or she has just "boarded a bus." The addict doesn't know where the bus is going or when it will leave or where it will stop. But by taking that first drink or drug, or engaging in whatever the addiction may be, he or she has purchased a ticket and has boarded the bus.

In early recovery from alcoholism and speed, Katie begins having difficulty sleeping. She decides she had never had a problem with marijuana, so she starts to use it to help her relax and sleep better. In time she becomes addicted to it and once again begins rationalizing, minimizing, and denying, hiding her addictive behavior, and not being honest with others. At a time of vulnerability, something negative happens in her life—maybe her boyfriend breaks up with her, her boss doesn't give her the raise she thinks she deserves, or it's her birthday and she thinks she should celebrate. It can be anything, and she quickly returns to her primary drugs of choice, alcohol and speed. By not accepting the need for total abstinence from all drugs and ignoring the possibility of multiple addictions, Katie has purchased her bus ticket.

Brain chemistry research shows that even after long periods of abstinence, once you ingest or engage in the addictive behavior or substance again, it is as if the brain loses the memory of recovery and the old "reward" memories are immediately reactivated.

While relapse is a common part of the disease, children need more information. As the recovering parent, you know relapse occurs for many reasons. In response to children's questions, it is very common for a parent to offer a succinct response of "it's a part of the disease." Children need more information than a dismissive answer. Your children need to hear you are taking responsibility for your recovery, and they want to know what you are doing differently that might preclude a future relapse. If you have experienced a relapse, you may not know exactly why, but you should have some insight. Offer your children any insights about what you did or did not do that may have influenced the relapse, and offer something positive you may have learned about yourself from the experience that will be helpful in preventing another. While you cannot promise there will never be a relapse, there is much you can do to lessen the likelihood.

The following are examples of common reasons for relapse and possible lessons to be learned.

- *You didn't initiate recovery.* Your original motivation to stop the addictive behavior was to accommodate or please another person. You didn't believe recovery was possible or necessary.
  Lesson learned: *I have to want recovery for myself for it to last.*
- *You didn't change your lifestyle.* You stopped the addictive behavior, but you kept all the aspects of daily life that didn't support recovery. You didn't learn to socialize with nondrinking or nonusing people. You continued to frequent the places that had supported your addiction. You did not attend self-help meetings.
  Lesson learned: *Recovery isn't just based on abstinence. I need to change other parts of my life as well.*
- *You didn't address significant emotional issues.* You didn't acknowledge painful experiences from your past or the profound feelings of fear, anger, and loneliness that surfaced in the absence of your addictive behavior. You didn't learn the skills to cope with ordinary daily feelings and the feelings that you've been carrying around for many years.
  Lesson learned: *I have to attend to healing from the trauma of painful experiences and feelings to sustain recovery.*
- *You didn't follow directions.* In recovery you were asked to do things that were scary or made you feel vulnerable, so your addictive thinking got tapped and you began to discount others' suggestions and started to dictate how you would do in recovery.
  Lesson learned: *Other recovering people have wisdom to offer me.*
- *You didn't exercise patience.* You maintained unrealistic expectations of how quickly you could regain your old life. You put together a

new life as if the addiction had not had a serious impact on your relationships and your skills.

Lesson learned: *I am not in control of other people, places, and things. I need to do the footwork, take the action, and have faith.*

- *You didn't learn to be accountable for self.* When you experienced problems you still looked first to others to assign blame without looking for your part in the situation. You tended to view other people, places, and things as the problem to be tackled, to be put into place.

Lesson learned: *When there is a problem or difficult situation, I need to look for my part in it and address my part. When I am not satisfied with the outcome, I need to let go of any resentments.*

- *You became overconfident.* As you began to feel better about yourself, you began to replay old messages such as, "My addiction is not as bad as other people's. I know what is best for me." You found yourself discounting what others were saying, only listening to yourself again.

Lesson learned: *I need to stay focused on the First Step of recovery, my powerlessness, and how my life has been unmanageable.*

Children frequently ask, "What should we do if you relapse?" This is a good question. The priority for all children is that they practice self-care. A nonadult child needs to have another adult whom he or she can talk to. An example of self-care for a young child could be refusing to go with the alcoholic when he or she is driving somewhere and appears to be under the influence. Or when parents are arguing, the child retreats to a different room. Self-care is telling another adult your thoughts and feelings.

Your grown children need the same messages to practice self-care and to set up strong boundaries. Your adult children are in a better position to practice nonenabling behaviors as you are in less of an authority position with them. It is unrealistic and inappropriate to expect a younger child to practice tough love one minute and interact with the parent as an authority figure the next.

It will be helpful to explain enabling to all of your children. Enabling is when they cover up, lie, or ignore your behavior and not say anything. Even young children enable. They hide your stash hoping you will not find it; they hide car keys hoping you will not leave the house and drive; they water down the booze or even pour it out. You need to tell them that you know they mean well, but that does not stop you from drinking or using.

You can ask adult children not to enable you. You know how they have enabled. Tell them what has happened in the past. It is possible they gave you money, even gave you some drugs. It is possible they bought the beer so you wouldn't drive to go get it. They may have lied for you to someone else. Tell them how that behavior just made it easier for you not to be responsible for yourself or not "hit bottom" so readily. It is also nonenabling if they tell you they know, or suspect, you are drinking or using.

Acknowledge that you are asking them to do something that you will most likely respond to in a discounting, possibly nonrational manner. But if they are able to engage in nonenabling behaviors, it may help you in the long run. It also helps them to know they are not keeping the truth silent.

Let all your children know you hope that a relapse will not occur, but if it does it is not because of anything they have done, said, not done, or not said. They did not cause the addiction, nor can they control it. Tell them again that you are accountable for your recovery, and you are the one who needs to learn how to live life sober.

This is a discussion for nonadult children.
After having shared about relapse and explained that you want them to take care of themselves if you relapse, ask your children if they can identify ways to do that. Dialogue and problem solve self-care. Being able to talk to another adult is very crucial. Ask them to identify two adults they would feel safe talking to. If they cannot, then you may make suggestions. This may be the other parent, it could be an extended family member, and it may be someone at school. Having a meaningful relationship with another adult prior to needing them at a time of crisis will make it more likely this child will reach out at a time of greater need. Children are not as apt to seek out an adult if they haven't previously developed a trusting and caring relationship. Support them in recognizing other adults as resources now and in the future.

Blackouts

As a recovering person, you may have experienced blackouts before you sobered up. If so, it is very possible that your children have interacted with you in this manner. You may need to explain that a blackout is a period of time when a person is under the influence of alcohol or drugs, yet is awake and interacting in the environment, possibly socially engaged. However, the memory of the experience is never recorded in the brain, and therefore the person is unable to remember what happened. This type of amnesia usually lasts several hours and in some instances a few days. An analogy that may be helpful in describing a blackout is a switch turning off one part of the brain and nothing is allowed to enter that part. When the switch comes back on, the part of the brain that was turned off remembers nothing.

It is important to note that lack of recall is not associated with only some behaviors. One does not experience blackouts only when being sexual or only when engaging in illegal behavior. A blackout has no external triggers. It is due solely to a biochemical response as a result of being under the influence of alcohol or drugs.

Blackouts are often "crazy making" for the family. Family members remember the experiences and they know the addict was present. They can't understand why the addict cannot remember. It doesn't make sense.

Family members have different experiences with blackouts. Shelley's dad didn't show up at her school play because he was out drinking and he forgot. He remembers leaving work, going to one of his favorite bars, watching the beginning of a ball game, and downing several beers, but that is all he remembers. He doesn't know whether or not he went to the event, or if he was drunk. He doesn't remember driving home or anything that occurred that evening. Shelley is deeply hurt and furious with her dad for disappointing her.

Many times Peter's father would call him "stupid" and "good for nothing" and the next day act like nothing had happened. His father had no recall of saying those things, and Peter was left sad and angry.

Children are often hurt by the addict's behavior while in a blackout, but it is possible for an interaction during a blackout to be nonhurtful. Tracy's mother attended some of her track meets, sat among the other parents, and appeared to have enjoyed it. While she didn't appear to be drunk or loaded at the time, the next day she had no recall of ever attending the event.

Whether or not the interaction during a blackout is painful, it is seldom discussed. Typically when the addicted person has had a blackout, he or she will not say, "Gee, I have no memory of last night, would you like to tell me about it?" The person doesn't want to ask about the "lost" time because that sets up an opportunity to look at his or her drinking or using, which creates an anxiety because the thought of not drinking or using is very frightening. The silence surrounding the blackout is due to a variety of feelings on everyone's part: the addict's guilt and fear; the spouse's anger and hopelessness; and the children's fear, embarrassment, guilt, and anger.

Often there is social reinforcement for drinking or using. The addict socializes with others who drink or use, and will boast about "not remembering" as if it were a badge of honor. Most people don't have a specific term to use for these "lost" episodes; they simply perceive them as something that happens to them while under the influence.

If you have experienced blackouts, your children may very well have some experiences that they need to talk about. You need to share with your children that you are responsible for your behavior. It is important that you and your children make the time to talk and listen to each other's experiences.

Have you had blackouts?

If so, tell your family and explain what they are. Encourage them to talk about any times they remember an experience when you later acted as if nothing had occurred. Whether or not they share an experience in which you were in a blackout, it will be an opportunity to open up a dialogue.

Recovery Practices

Generally, children aren't adverse to their parents going to Twelve Step meetings or other forms of aftercare and support. They are simply curious as to how the meetings are helpful and why there is a need to continue going to meetings long after the addictive behavior has stopped.

Your children may have negative feelings about you going to meetings because they want to see more of you and they think the meetings are going to conflict with getting the attention they would like. It's not that your children need you to do special things with them; they just want to have you home and attentive to them.

If your children are young and living at home, it can be difficult to find the time to be home with them and at the same time attend the number of meetings that you need. Children will be more accepting of Twelve Step meetings as they begin to realize that you are going to be more available to them than you were before. Talk with them and commit yourself to being available to them at preplanned times each week.

It may be that your children are adults and not in need of your daily attention. In this case it may be easier to plan times with them without any conflict in attending to your recovery practices.

Michael, whom we have followed in this book, was in a strange situation. He didn't think his children were aware of his addiction or his recovery. He had two concerns: should he tell them at all? And, if he did, what information would be age appropriate for his young children?

Michael's young children may have felt the strain between their parents due to Michael's addiction, but they did not see him use alcohol or drugs, nor see him when he was under the influence. Michael is wondering how to tell them about his Twelve Step programs when he and his wife think the children have been oblivious to the problem. He doesn't want to restrict his recovery meetings to times that his children would not notice his absence, nor does he want to lie about his whereabouts.

It is important for Michael and his wife to tell the children that he attends AA meetings and why. Rather than having an in-depth discussion, addiction can be talked about very simply. "While most people don't have a problem with drinking, in the past Daddy did, so he decided to not drink at all. He goes to meetings with other people who also have had a drinking problem. This helps him feel good about himself and it is a way of taking care of him and us." If it is presented in a matter-of-fact manner, and as if it is no problem to them, they are very likely to readily accept the explanation. They don't have a need to know about the wreckage, nor does he need to share any more detail. As the kids get older, and as it is appropriate in natural conversation, more can be shared.

After Michael told his children that he has been addicted to alcohol and drugs and that he goes to Twelve Step recovery meetings, his children wanted to know if he has to go to these meetings for the rest of his life.

What would happen if he misses the meetings? Michael tells his children how much he loves them, but without sobriety he wouldn't be able to show that love. Meetings help him to stay sober. He explains to them that nothing bad will happen if he misses a meeting; he just doesn't want to make a habit of missing them. He tells them that while he has certain meetings he goes to more than others, there will be times when the family will take priority and he can attend other meetings.

Dina's young children, ages six and nine, readily accept her going to Al-Anon meetings. They believe these meetings help their mother feel better, and she smiles more. But her older children are confused as to why she would continue to go to Al-Anon if their father were to become sober. She explains to her teenagers that she has spent a lot of time focusing on their father's addictive behavior, often enabling him, losing sight of other priorities. By attending meetings she feels better about herself, and she believes that makes her a better person. She also thinks it helps her be a better parent. She finds she isn't preoccupied with their father so much; she can focus more on them. She can see the good in life, and she is a better mother and enjoys being a mother a lot more. She is not so depressed, angry, or unpredictable.

Dillon told his young adult children that he found the peer support and structure of the Twelve Steps was his path to staying abstinent. He said he could see the principles of recovery in action at meetings. There was something bigger than himself in those meetings. They allowed him to be humble about who he was, to be willing to follow direction, and to stay focused on his priority of not drinking or using. He reminded his children that being humble, following direction, and being clean and sober were things he could never have found or maintained on his own.

Kyle's dad, Neil, explained to him that even though he is now sober for three years and Kendra, his wife, sober for eleven years, they continue going to meetings for two reasons: (1) going to meetings keeps them more honest with themselves, and (2) going to meetings allows them to give to newcomers what had been given to them in their early months and years of recovery. He explained to Kyle that addiction is not like other illnesses that are predominantly physical, such as pneumonia, where you are initially treated and cured. Abstinence was only the first step in addiction treatment and recovery.

Neil talked about his addiction with his son and explained how in his addiction he did things he didn't like about himself. "I became dishonest, I didn't listen or respect others. I was manipulative and always tried to control situations. Being abstinent didn't suddenly take that away. I practiced those hurtful behaviors for many years prior to getting sober and even after I was sober. I go to meetings because the Twelve Steps teach me how to be accountable for my behavior and not blame others, as well as how to be patient and tolerant of others and myself. I am not so judgmental or critical. I stay sober in part because I am an honest person today. It has been difficult for me to be honest, but the Steps help me. This program helps me to like myself as a person, which makes me more fun to be around, but mostly it makes me a better person."

He went on to explain that addiction is a disease that will always be with him and recovery is practiced one day at a time. "That is another reason why meetings are so important. They are great reminders that my addiction is one drink or drug away. Meetings keep me vigilant and help me not become complacent."

Kendra shared with Kyle, "Going to meetings is like putting money into a savings account and earning interest. Going to meetings is my 'recovery interest.' If something happens that makes me feel insecure or threatens my sobriety, I can draw on my experiences of listening to what others have said about how they have coped with different situations. This consistently reinforces my desire not to drink, to take life a day at a time, and to realize there is no life challenge that is a threat to my sobriety today."

Kyle was curious about the spiritual part of his father's and stepmother's recovery. He wondered if his alcoholic mother would have to take on some "religion" in order to become sober. His father and stepmother explained to him that Twelve Step programs offer a broad concept of spirituality, even accepting atheists, those who do not believe in a God. They explained that Twelve Step programs are not based on any specific religion, but in a belief in a Higher Power, a power greater than oneself that individuals could name for themselves. They also told Kyle that his mother had other options for recovery, that Twelve Step programs were not the only resource available. They explained that some people found a commitment or a recommitment to their faith that provided the foundation for recovery through a church rather than a Twelve Step group.

Aware that Kyle thought his mother would not get sober if she was a part of a program that had a spiritual or religious basis, they told him that some people seek out counseling and keep it as their primary resource and foundation to recovery, and that in some communities there are self-help meetings that are not spiritually based. They reminded him that any resistance his mother had to getting sober was most likely because she wasn't ready to stop her drinking or using yet, rather than there being a problem with the potential resources.

James's son accused his father of just switching addictions from alcoholism to Twelve Step meetings. James told his son, "I learned that I should go to meetings like I used to drink. Since I drank daily, I need to be in meetings daily. My disease was not just when I was under the influence. My disease was the way I thought about the world, and myself, and the way I acted that out. They say in the beginning go to ninety meetings in ninety days, and I go every day because this is what has worked for so many people."

James embraced the spiritual part of recovery from his early days of sobriety. "All I ever believed in was me, me, me. I controlled and hurt others. I gave no thought to anyone else or how my behavior impacted them. I was my Higher Power; the bottle was my Higher Power. Something got through to me in recovery. I quit believing that I know best, that I am the center of the universe. I no longer doubt there is a Higher Power. Some people believe their Higher Power is God, but all the program asks of us is to recognize a Higher Power as a power greater than ourselves.

"I know now that by turning my will and love over to the care of a Higher Power I am no longer hurtful to others. I am more patient—yes, me patient. Not great, but better. I am not nearly so scared, and I have been running scared and angry my whole life. I am not angry at the world, and even though I am not thrilled with myself yet, I am not the same person I was. Today I put one foot in front of the other, I do the action, and I have faith in my Higher Power. I couldn't get sober by myself and you know how I tried. I even tried meetings before, but I fought them. This time I knew I had to surrender to my Higher Power and quit being the one in charge."

When children are curious or critical about what they refer to as "religious stuff," they are usually reacting to a concept foreign to them. They may perceive a spiritual or religious person as being moralistic or "holier than thou" and unapproachable. Since you were not available to them when you were drinking and/or using, your new spirituality may be perceived as something that will still make you unavailable or distant.

As you give your children time and attention and focus on their needs, not just yours, they will begin to be supportive of what you need to do for your recovery. The key here is a recovery slogan, *keep it simple*. Keep your conversations and your expectations simple.

In closing this chapter, I would like to share a story about children's willingness to accept how recovery works for the adults in their lives. Ginny and her six-year-old granddaughter, Heidi, were in a grocery store. Ginny, who has been sober for more than twenty years, was being admittedly grouchy with Heidi. As they came up to the checkout stand, Heidi looked at the clerk who was overhearing their conversation and said, "Please, don't mind my grandma, she needs an AA meeting."

Chapter 5

Early Recovery
and Making Amends

If there ever is a time to practice letting go, it is when talking to your kids. —Liz

Terror, Bewilderment, Frustration, and Despair are called the "Four Horsemen" in *Alcoholics Anonymous,* the Big Book.[1] Typically these emotions refer to the addicted person's relationship with the addiction. They also describe the experiences of many children living in an addictive family system. They also give names to the feelings of many recovering parents attempting to develop healthier relationships with their kids.

The terror is sometimes quite obvious in the parent who says, "I barely know my kids, why would they want to have a relationship with me?" The bewilderment may sound like, "Who are these kids? What are they about? What will I offer them? I am barely an adult myself." The frustration often occurs when the relationship doesn't develop as quickly as you want. The despair may occur when you feel out of control in the parent department, or think you can never do enough to make things right. This chapter will offer you a path to walk through some of these experiences.

Where there is loss, there will be tears; where there is loss, there will be anger.

Healing the Pain

Loss is integral to addiction; it permeates all relationships. The addict, spouse, and children of any and all ages experience loss when there is addiction in the family. For the children, there is much that doesn't get said that needs to be said in order for them to feel loved; there is much that doesn't occur that needs to occur for closeness and intimacy. On the flip side, there is much that *is* said, and that *does* occur that strips the family of trust, safety, and respect.

As a consequence, talking about addiction will bring up feelings that need to be discussed directly to promote the possibility of healing the relationships. Due to the children's history of not trusting they would be heard, and without the practice of sharing feelings in a constructive manner, this process begins gingerly. Yet it does begin and there are many families who are testaments to the gifts of recovery that come with family healing.

If the addicted parent has had the opportunity to attend a treatment center with a family program that included children, it is possible that the children have been exposed to the process of sharing honestly about how they experienced their parent's behavior. If this has not occurred, the possibility of using a counselor to facilitate the initial communication may still be an option. Attending Al-Anon for the older teenagers and adult children, or Al-Ateen for the younger and middle-aged teenagers, is another resource that is very helpful in supporting family dialogue. If the children are still school age, it is possible that the school may have resources for children raised with addiction, and it is quite common for a staff person to be available within the school or the school district.

Dillon, who had not raised his children but was now their only parent, felt too intimidated to begin this process himself. He was relieved that his treatment program offered his adult children an avenue to begin to share their thoughts and feelings.

Kendra and her husband felt that by their use of Twelve Step programs and by introducing their teenagers to Al-Ateen, they could create a sense of safety and structure within the family to strengthen a communication process.

Dina's children, who are still subject to a father active in his disease, differ in their ability to talk openly about their feelings. Dina's recovery has made it possible for her to listen to her son vent his many feelings, but her fourteen-year-old daughter has begun to make disparaging comments about her father in front of the younger children. She has begun to stay out past appropriate times, is surly with Dina, and is isolating at home in her room. Dina found herself validating her daughter's right to be angry, but also validating what her daughter didn't own: her hurt, embarrassment, and fear. Dina had to set stronger limits around her daughter's behavior. By being more engaged with her younger children and finding more social support for them with their friends' parents, she saw them acting happier and practicing better self-care.

James's son, now thirty, may very well have his own burgeoning alcohol problem. He expresses happiness that his father is getting sober, but he doesn't want much to do with James right now. Talking privately with a family counselor at a treatment program, he expresses his anger. "Where was my dad when I was fifteen years old? I needed him then, I don't need him now. My life is already screwed up."

While many children are angry about what has occurred in the past, some children are so grateful and want so much for their parent to stay in recovery that they will go to any lengths to avoid conflict. They don't want to do or say anything that will upset their parent. This behavior gives the appearance of letting go of old angers when actually it is often a symptom of anger avoidance, based on fear of greater rejection.

Dillon's daughter, Jackie, is an example of someone who cannot own any anger due to her fear of rejection. She was raised by her alcoholic mother and a rageful stepfather, whose use of anger was highly inappropriate and abusive. When her mother died she went to live with her chemically dependent father. When he became sober two years later, all she could say is that he has been a wonderful father to her. She has never allowed herself to recognize any anger toward her father. When her mother died, the only significant adult figure in her life was her father, who had never been blatantly hurtful toward her. She believed her father was wonderful and even more so since he was sober and wanted to spend time with her.

If Jackie continues to deny her anger and idealize a father who, while not abusive, had emotionally abandoned her in his disease, she is at risk to continue a pattern of dismissing her feelings while idealizing those who are hurtful or abandoning toward her. She will maintain a high tolerance for hurtful behavior, which sets her up for victim-like relationships. If Jackie can own the pain and the anger, she has an opportunity to find that in owning her truth, no matter what it is, she can be heard, valued, and loved. This is a life-transforming lesson that can be learned in a recovery process.

Kendra's stepson is in a precarious situation. He lives with two recovering alcoholics, but on weekends he visits his mother, who is still active in her disease. He needs all three adults in his life but is confused about his loyalties. Why didn't his dad go back to his mother once he became sober and help her get sober instead of marrying someone else? Why can't his mother get sober if his dad and stepmother did? Doesn't she love him? He is angry and isn't sure who to be angry at. He doesn't want to be angry with his mother or he might not get to visit her. How can he be angry with his dad? After all, he doesn't drink anymore. And his stepmother doesn't drink either, and she wants him in her life, so why doesn't his own mother act like that?

It is very painful for the addicted parent to put him- or herself in the shoes of a family member. This is exacerbated even more so if the parent grew up with addiction. It can be difficult to be empathetic to your own children if you are defending against the pain of your own childhood. Follow the direction of your counselor, your sponsor, and those who are supporting you in your recovery, but realize that, at some point, you will benefit greatly by doing what is called "family of origin" work. In the meantime, you need to know your children have reasons for whatever feelings they are experiencing. The family has the right to be angry, confused, sad, or whatever they are feeling about the hurtful behavior and the absence of consistent loving behavior over the years.

Affirmations can often be helpful at a time of vulnerability. From the list below, circle the affirmations and/or name others that could help you embrace conversations with your children.

I am a person my child can trust.

I am a loving parent.

I am perfect in my imperfections.

We all have our different realities.

I am a good and worthwhile person and parent.

I create a safe environment for my children.

The possibility of closeness only occurs by taking risks.

Others: _____

A Child's Many Feelings

It can be uncomfortable to look at the pain an addiction causes a child. Nevertheless, it can also be helpful to validate these feelings for the child. The following lists can give you some ideas about what your child has faced.

Fear:
- when Mom and Dad have a fight
- that Dad will be rageful again
- that I will say the wrong thing and Mom will leave the house and I won't know when she will be back

Sadness:
- for the times Mom or Dad didn't show up at an important event
- that I'm disappointing my parents because I'm not good enough
- when Mom took too many pills and had to go to the hospital

Embarrassment:
- when Mom slurred her words in front of my friends
- when Dad got too friendly with one of my girlfriends
- when Dad got drunk at the family reunion

Guilt:
- for being angry with my mom or dad
- for not wanting to spend time with my mom or dad
- for making life so difficult for my mother

Anger:
- about things always being so messed up
- about all the lying
- about all the broken promises and false promises

Hopelessness:
- that nothing will ever really change

Nate, thirteen, told me about an incident when his father passed out in the front yard after swearing obscenities at Nate's friends. This scene was witnessed by friends, neighbors, Nate, his eleven-year-old sister, and his mother. Dad had staggered into the front yard in his underclothes, swearing obscenities. After creating a commotion that drew many neighbors to their porches, he passed out in the yard. Many of the witnesses to this scene gathered in the yard and simply circled Nate's father until a sheriff arrived and took him away.

I asked Nate how that was for him, to hear his father swearing and yelling at friends, being seen in his underclothes, passing out, and being taken away by a sheriff. Nate responded, "What do you mean, how was that?" I was trying not to put words into his mouth, but I said, "How did that make you feel?" He responded, "What do you mean, how did I feel?" I repeated myself and said, "What did you feel when you saw and heard this?" He was unable to respond to the question.

I have learned that sometimes we ask people to do things they don't yet have the skills to do. It was possible that Nate never developed the ability to identify feelings, or at some point, lost that ability. We focused on other things in our sessions, and after a time, when there was more trust between us, I asked him to create a list of feelings people have. He created a list of seventeen feelings. I then asked him to check those feelings he has experienced in his thirteen years of life. He checked twelve of them. There were five feelings he believes others have felt but he hasn't: loneliness, anger, fear, sadness, and embarrassment. I then asked, "Nate, is there a reason other people have those five feelings but you never do?" He responded bluntly and poignantly, "Maybe because I have to be tough and they don't."

Parents often have no idea of the range or depth of feelings children are experiencing. In part this is due to the fact that parents are caught up in their own world and while that is occurring, children learn how to minimize, rationalize, and discount their feelings. This is what the child does in order to protect him- or herself. One recovering father shared the following thoughts:

After I was sober a couple of years, and my kids saw that I was staying sober, I told them, all young adults, that at some point they may need to get angry with me for making them grow up with an addiction. They weren't acting or sounding angry, but I found I needed to do my work around the fact that I grew up with addiction and I had a lot of anger. I didn't act or sound angry either, but I certainly found ways to medicate.

You are now in a position to take responsibility for doing your part in connecting with your children. It may begin in the form of verbal amends, it may be making behavioral amends, or it may be both. But before I talk about amends, it is helpful to address guilt and shame.

Guilt and Shame

Addicted parents frequently act outside of their value systems, have misplaced priorities, and feel guilty for being hurtful toward others. Guilt is a feeling of regret and remorse about your behavior, things you have done and not done. If your children would just say, "It is okay, it wasn't that bad," then you wouldn't have to recognize the impact of your behavior on another. Those words would give you permission not to feel so bad about yourself; maybe you aren't such a bad person.

The truth is you are guilty. You have done things for which you feel regret and remorse. That is what happens with addiction. The addiction has been central to your life and in that process the many other important parts of your life are neglected. In addiction you do and say things for which, now that you are clean and sober, you are very remorseful. You would do anything to take back the pain your behavior has brought to others.

Many recovering parents seek forgiveness, not for their guilt but for what has turned into shame. A helpful distinction between the two is that guilt is the feeling of regret and remorse when you have made mistakes; shame encompasses many painful feelings that come with the belief that you are unworthy, not of value, a bad person. Unhealthy shame is a negative belief that keeps you in a "less than" position, the belief that who you are is unlovable and inadequate.

In recovery, it is vital for you to embrace that while you may have done things that were bad and certainly hurtful to others, you are not bad. You are not unworthy; you are not unlovable; you are not less than another. The key to resolving feelings of guilt is to be accountable for your behavior, stay accountable for your behavior, and forgive yourself.

You cannot afford to let shame haunt you even though you may berate yourself for many mistakes. You ask, how can I forgive myself? How can I expect my children to ever be willing to trust me when I behaved the way I did? What kind of a parent would bring home one sexual partner after another, without any regard for the children? What kind of mother would expose an unborn baby to alcohol or drugs? What kind of a father would ignore his children during their growing-up years?

Letting go of shame occurs, in part, with genuinely accepting your addiction as a disease. You would not have made the decisions or behaved in a manner that hurt your children and the others that you love had you not been acting out addictive thinking and behavior. You would have had greater choices. The shameful behaviors further establish the powerlessness and the unmanageability of the disease. The behaviors belong to the disease.

Amends

Twelve Step programs offer a path to address one's guilt. Step Eight suggests that you make a list of all persons you have harmed and become willing to make amends. Step Nine suggests that you make amends except when to do so would cause injury.

To lessen the pain and be more accountable, it is most wise that you discuss your intentions with a sponsor. Feedback is important and your sponsor is in a position to talk with you about the appropriateness of the timing, etc.

Amends come in the form of both verbal apologies and new behavior. Be careful with your expectations. Amends are for the amend maker—it makes you a healthier recovering person. You are being responsible and accountable. You make amends to be a better parent. Should your children genuinely forgive you, it is a blessing, but this usually takes time and is the result of your new behaviors. Adolescent and adult-age children are less likely to be accepting of amends in your early recovery, as they need to see the recovery unfold.

When an addicted parent hurts and angers a child by his or her addictive behavior, the reaction of the child may fester over a period of time, possibly lasting and increasing to the time when the addict becomes clean and sober. So when the addicted parent begins the recovery process there often exists a significant amount of residual feelings. These feelings do not disappear with a single act of contrition or amends. Just as the addict's hurtful behavior was practiced over time, forgiveness will be practiced over a period of time as well. That doesn't mean you don't apologize and even make some amends, but it does mean that it is important to see verbal amends as more than a onetime event.

While you cannot take back the hurt or anger your behavior may have caused, children do need to hear that you are sorry. Speak to what you did and did not do for which you are sorry. You need to be specific and only speak to that which pertains to them.

 The following are sentence stems that can be helpful language to offer verbal amends.

I am responsible for_____ and for that I feel_____.
Or,
I have been hurtful toward you when I _____
and for that I feel _____.
Some examples follow.
"I am responsible for not making my child support payments, and you and your brother suffered because of that, and for that I am deeply ashamed. I have been hurtful toward you when I was not available for so many of your activities growing up, and for that I feel very sad."
Or,
I am sorry for _____.
Some examples follow.
"I am sorry for not seeing you on the weekends that were mine to see you."
"I am sorry for embarrassing you in front of your friends when I got drunk."
If you want to make verbal amends, list each of your children by name and write out your amends. Share this with a sponsor or counselor for feedback.

Should you make amends, some children will immediately try to take care of you, diminishing the behavior that was hurtful to them to make you feel better about yourself. It is important that you let them know you don't need them to take care of you; you are taking care of yourself now. Taking care of yourself means taking responsibility for your behavior. Let your children know nothing bad is happening when you are experiencing pain, hurt, etc. You are able to tolerate those feelings. This will sound foreign to them, particularly coming from you, but it is important these words be said.

Some children will quickly dismiss you with, "Okay Dad. Okay Mom, can I leave now?"

If you are finished speaking, know you said what you needed to say and it needs time to sink in. You don't necessarily need a discussion. Remember this is not your only time for making amends; other times can be created or will come naturally. Here's what Trisha had to say about her experience:

> *I found that my daughter wanted me to apologize out loud and she wanted to talk about it and then she wanted me to change. With the boys, they didn't want me to do anything but change and then they would know. I didn't have to tell them.*

Some children will barely listen because for them apologies are cheap. They have heard too many apologies, only to have you fall back on your promises, your words, your intent. While you may begin with verbal amends, know it is your behavior that will make the ultimate difference in their lives.

Here are examples of behavioral amends:

- When you are invited to your granddaughter's birthday party, instead of making excuses for why you can't come, you show up on time and stay until the end.
- When your son or daughter comes in after dinner excited about something that happened, rather than ignoring him or her you stop what you are doing and listen. Act as if nothing else is more important than listening to your child.
- One of your children brings home a notice that there is a school event where an adult chaperone is needed. In the past you never noticed the request or made time. Today you not only volunteer, you initiate finding out about the upcoming event.
- You go on a camping trip with your kids, a trip that all of you plan

together. Previously, you always promised to take them camping but ultimately created excuses and did not go.

Children need your behavior to say they are of value to you. It is your behavior that will make the ultimate difference in their lives.

Children also need to know you are thinking of other family members. Some children ignore their own pain, feeling more empathetic toward a sibling or other parent. Children may wonder how far reaching in the family your accountability extends. This is a normal part of their struggling with trust. It can be very healing for your children to know you have remorse about your behavior toward their siblings, their other parent, etc. It is not usually advisable to be specific regarding other family members, but you can tell them you are quite sorry about your behavior.

As the family becomes more trusting, each person will likely become more honest. Over time you may realize how your behavior has been even more irresponsible and hurtful to those you love. As a consequence, as recovery progresses, there may be more guilt than there was in the beginning. With that comes the opportunity for spontaneous amends.

Making amends, verbal or behavioral, is about being accountable to your children.

Children often espouse words of forgiveness without understanding or feeling true forgiveness. They are understanding of your addiction and feel love toward you, but usually they need to be able to speak the truth of their experiences before they feel a genuine forgiveness. This takes time and healing.

Self-forgiveness

Accountability and responsibility are not the same as forgiveness. You need to be accountable and responsible when you have hurt others and make amends, if possible. But then you need to forgive yourself for having made the mistakes, for having blundered in your humanness. You may always regret what happened, but you need to address your toxic shame through self-forgiveness. Forgiving means letting go of the shame.

The opposite of "to forgive" is "to condemn." Whatever you condemn, you don't accept. When you continue to condemn yourself, you are not accepting who you are, your humanness, or your addiction. You, more than anyone, need to understand that addiction is addiction, that it casts a shadow and influences your behaviors, even when you are not immediately under the influence of the substance or behavior. Remind yourself that when you were in the throes of an addiction, it had a life of its own, causing you to act outside your value system and do things that hurt others. Addiction has been a way of life that kept you self-centered, operating from shame and delusional thinking.

When feeling guilty, the need to punish yourself is a learned and internalized behavior. You were not born with an internal judge of your badness. Instead of hanging on to hurt, judgment, and negativity, you deserve to allow yourself to experience self-forgiveness.

For most people forgiveness is something that occurs gradually. This is true for forgiveness of self as much as it is for forgiveness of others. As you do the work of healing, forgiveness will naturally begin to manifest itself in your life. Pain can be replaced by a deeply felt spiritual acceptance. With every tear that is shed and every cry of anguish that is released, the heart is opened for forgiveness. Ultimately it is your own powerful spirit that will heal you.

Am I willing to forgive myself?   Yes   No   Not Sure
If you cannot answer yes, whom can you talk to, or what do you need to do to become more willing to forgive yourself?

In conclusion, try to remember that every time you make amends to one of your children by verbally apologizing and changing, you make progress toward forgiving yourself.

Chapter 6

New Ways of Relating

My two girls were only nine and ten when I got clean. I have a lot to make up for. I started taking diet pills when I was a teenager, and it quickly became a full-blown addiction. I made my first suicide attempt at age twenty-three. My poor husband, he really didn't have any idea what he was getting into when he married me. But maybe on some level he did, as his mother was frequently sick and used a lot of pills. Anyway, literally everybody in my family was addicted to one substance or another, and there have been some violent deaths too. My own daughters saw me nearly die in two overdoses. I have spent most of the last three years doing a lot of recovery work and gradually rebuilding my girls' trust.

In my last treatment program, I sat with them, their father, and a counselor and told them I was sorry for all that they have had to see. I was sorry for not having been a good mom to them. I told them I loved them very much and my behavior was not a reflection of what I felt for them. I told them I was going to work very hard to never again take pills or drink— that in our family this is poison. All of the women have been addicted to pills, so I want them to get this message. Since then I haven't said a whole lot directly to them; mostly I try to be home when they get home from school and participate in their school events. They need to trust me before my words will mean much. But it has been better this past year; we laugh a lot more together. —Michelle

The ways in which you are able to be there for your children will be as vast as the number of relationships that exist. It begins by giving your children both time and attention. Listening to them is more important than talking to them in many situations. This chapter will relate some personal stories that may offer you direction and hope. It is important for you to accept that other people do not necessarily do their recovery in your time frame. You

71

need to take responsibility for your part and practice the art of letting go. As one father said, "My children have God as a protector. He is not just for me."

Reconnection: Offering Validation

The addicted parent needs to be willing to let his or her children know they have the right to their many feelings and be specific in validating the children's experiences. "I haven't been home when I should have been, and you have all the reasons in the world to be angry." "I have spoken to you very critically. I have said demeaning things to you. You have the right to be angry." "I have not made special time with you." "I wasn't there for your graduation," or "I wasn't there when your daughter was born." "I showed up for the big events, but wasn't there for the daily part of your life. That had to hurt."

By being specific your children are able to hear that you genuinely grasp their pain and their reality. In essence, their emotional experiences need your validation.

Validation of your children's feelings needs to occur repetitively over time. The first few times your children will not trust this communication. A child may think, "Okay, does this mean I am not supposed to have any more feelings just because you are clean and sober and you want a new relationship with me?" Trust comes with time. Work your program of recovery and be consistent with your new behavior toward your children.

Tips for Listening to Your Child

- Make eye contact.
- Don't interrupt.
- Keep the focus on the child.
- Validate and accept his or her right to feelings.
- Avoid body language, words, or looks that demonstrate judgment.
- Don't ask the child to defend or explain why he or she is feeling a certain way. Asking a child to justify feelings can suggest that you won't accept his or her feelings unless there is a good enough reason for them.

- Respect the fact that he or she may not want to talk about something at that moment.

Identify each of your children by name.
What feelings do each of them readily own?
What feelings do you think each of them has that they aren't talking about?

Reconnection: Being There

Jennifer, mother of three adult children, says this about being present in her children's lives:

My kids were all adults by the time I got sober. It was my youngest daughter who asked and pleaded for me to get help. Now she is the one who is struggling the most as a consequence of my not being there for her during her growing-up years. She is very angry with me. I am an adult child, which does give me some perspective into my children's lives. All I think I can do is show up in her life as much as she is willing to allow. The other kids need me to show up as well. One of them now attends my AA anniversary nights. I haven't shared with them the wreckage of my past; they saw it; they lived it. I am sad that we cannot be closer as I love them and will be there for them as they let me.

James's son and daughter are grown and live outside of the home. His son is in the middle of a divorce and remains distant from him. James's initial inroad to rebuilding a relationship with his son and his grandchildren was offering to help with the logistics of picking up the grandkids from their mother's house and getting them home. To begin to rebuild the relationship with his daughter, James asks her for the time to share about the family addiction and wants to know how it was for her to live with his addiction while growing up.

Dillon knew how to include his adult son in his drinking life—they drank together—but how could he include his son in his sober life? While in treatment he invited his son to family week and his son, who may have a drinking problem as well, received some good education about the genetics of alcoholism and family dynamics. Dillon put no limits on whether or not his son drank; rather, he focused on spending time with him. Dillon began to ask his son to ball games and included his other recovering friends and their children. His son has some expertise in computers so Dillon asked him for some assistance in setting up his system. When his son was moving, Dillon made himself available to unload boxes. He was going to be patient and have faith that the opportunity to be more specific with amends would present itself naturally as more trust evolved between them.

Dillon's daughter, Jackie, also attended family week, which started them talking about topics that had previously not been discussed, such as her feelings about him over the years and being subject to parental alcoholism. He acknowledged his absence in her life and that he had not protected her in some important ways. While she was temperate with her feelings, he let her know that whatever feelings she would come to share he would be able to listen to and acknowledge. He would begin to be a "show up" father.

Earlier we heard the story of Kendra's stepson, Kyle, who is now living with two recovering parents, Kendra and his father, Neil. Neil raised Kyle during his active alcoholism but left the marriage after becoming sober. Kyle, age eight, stayed with his drug- and alcohol-addicted mother for the next four years. Kyle doesn't remember much about his father's addiction. Neil went to court for custody of Kyle and received it when Kyle was twelve. Kyle remembers that if his mother had chosen to go for treatment, as the judge recommended, then the court would not have placed Kyle in his father's home. Kyle was willing enough to live with his father, as his mother had a boyfriend and a new baby and it did not seem she was too interested in his being there.

While Kyle likes his new home, he is confused and angry. Kyle has been a witness to the wreckage of addiction. He needs a stable family life where he is allowed to be the child, not the primary caretaker. He needs adults who will talk openly about addiction as a disease and not focus on his mother being a bad mother.

For now, Kyle will need help to stop personalizing his mother's behavior as a statement about him or her love for him. That is a lot to ask of a young person, but with supporting adults in his life consistently offering protection and guidance, Kyle can develop skills to cope with his very sick mother. In time Kyle's father can begin to talk more specifically about his own addiction and recovery and help Kyle to find the answers to his questions about his parents' alcoholism.

Don't let your children manipulate you by pointing out your past actions.
   Don't expect consistency in their behaviors. In time, however, communication can open up the perceptions of each family member.

Addressing the Wreckage of the Past

Wreckage of the past refers to the aspects of your life that are negatively affected by the addiction. It includes relationships, physical health, finances, and individual mental health. While there are exceptions, it is commonly acknowledged by recovering addicts that they (the addict) were the last ones to recognize the addiction. Usually, by the time an addict recognizes the addiction, everyone in the family is already aware, as well as neighbors and co-workers. Those close to the addict are usually the ones most aware. To think that your children are oblivious to your addiction or the related behaviors is usually blatant denial.

If your children have grown up with any active addiction, the wreckage of the past has caused conflict, pain, and possibly anger. Your children may very well have been dealing with those feelings alone. In an attempt to compensate for the past hurt, you may not think to talk openly about what is occurring. You become overprotective by not sharing with your children that which does concern them. With honesty and a consistent display of recovery behavior, you can convey to your children that any concerns and problems they have will be addressed. You need to invite them to ask questions; you need to respond to those questions when your behavior has impacted their lives.

As difficult as this is to believe for parents, children more likely than not know when secrets are in the house. So many times I have sat with parents who are struggling about whether or not to tell their children something they think their children need to know, but don't think they do. To their surprise, most often, the children knew. If they did not know the specifics, they knew the generalities. Sometimes they didn't know everything; sometimes they didn't know much, but they knew there was a secret.

There are very good reasons to talk with your children:

- To offer validation. Having their unspoken perceptions validated takes away the "craziness" of knowing but not knowing. Validation diminishes the additional shame and anxiety that come with secrecy.
- To lessen the opportunity for surprise discovery. It is likely others who know about your addiction will tell them, such as a sibling, someone in the community, or possibly the media. Were you engaged in some behavior and is it possible your name or even your picture may be in the paper? Might someone at school have a parent who would tell his or her child something that your child might hear through the school grapevine? Your thoughtful sharing can be offered in a healthy manner to counteract a mean-spirited or otherwise simply thoughtless act. Do not share with one child what you aren't willing to share with another. To ask children to keep family secrets from each other is addictive behavior. Many parents have had greater difficulty in their parent/child relationship when they did not share some information and their adolescent or adult child found out on his or her own.
- To broaden the understanding of the ramifications of addiction, setting the stage for the potential to stop the cycle of addiction in your family.

How much should you tell your children? As a general guideline, children need to know information that has influence on their lives.

The wreckage of the past that influences children is most often about finances, health, their parents' relationship, and possibly legal issues. If there is a financial impact in which children could feel the consequences, they need to have information. Does losing your job affect their plans for college, or the promised new computer, or bicycle? Do your legal expenses get in the way of their going to summer camp?

If there is a question about the stability of the marriage, children need to know. If a separation or divorce is being discussed or planned, adolescent and adult-age children can usually cope with the truth that they already suspect anyway. For example, you could say, "We are discussing a divorce, and if that happens we will do what we can not to disrupt your schooling. We will work it out so we both stay active in the parenting. We will let you know if we make that decision."

If you and your partner are making efforts to stabilize the relationship, it can be helpful for the children to hear that as well. It may also surprise them to hear you say, "Your father and I are working to keep this marriage together. Should we not be able to do that, we will work it out the best we can so your life is disrupted as little as possible."

The key to the conversation is to offer your children information that is pertinent to how their life will be impacted. Use discretion. Children do not need to be kept abreast of the minutiae of the day-to-day process. They are not confidants for you to use for support or problem solving. You need to have others outside of the family system to turn to for feedback or support.

Children are not confidants for you to use for support or problem solving. You need to have others outside of the family system to turn to for feedback or support.

If you have health issues that impact your children, they need to know. For example, if you are giving yourself intravenous injections of interferon for hepatitis C and hiding it from your children, tell them you have a chronic disease for which you are receiving treatment. This type of secrecy can be more damaging than the truth. What your children want to hear is how you are taking care of yourself with any health issue. Again, if presented in a matter-of-fact manner, and if you are getting medical help, this will balance the fear that comes with hearing the diagnosis.

The following is a story that reminds us that every parent will have specific individual considerations, and there is no one way in which to parent.

Lynne was diagnosed with hepatitis C two years ago. The disease is a direct result of her drug history. She has two daughters, eleven and fourteen, and she has chosen not to tell them at this time. She said:

At first I knew I needed to be able to process the information before I was comfortable talking about it with anyone other than my husband and a few close adult friends. I was practicing good health; I stopped smoking when the girls were babies.

I have been clean since before my kids were born. I have been forthright about being an alcoholic and drug addict and just as forthright about being in recovery. But I have no need for them to know the details of my drug usage. I don't see how that is helpful to them either. Why should my children have to cope with this information when their daily reality is something different? Every day they get older and become more mature. So when they are older I will share in more detail.

In my case they are not likely to find out about the hepatitis C and if they do, or were to ask me directly, I would tell them. If I become sick and need to take medications I will tell them. But right now I take no medications nor am I under any treatment. And should that happen I would emphasize the positive reports from doctors. When I researched hepatitis C on the Internet, so much of the data available was negative and frightening, and yet my experience, and that of many I know, is not what is available.

I handle my parenting on a need-to-know basis. As a parent I make decisions, and sometimes I am not really sure about the decisions. I could come to regret this one, but at the moment, I am making my decisions as best as I can.

But sometimes the wreckage of the past is not so blatant. Jeff shared:

My children have grown up watching me be active in Twelve Step meetings. My recovery is just common knowledge, and I am proud of my recovery. I have never shared with them the details of my usage, not the types of drugs, stories, or frequency with which I used. I have been a hard-core drug user; I didn't want to diminish myself in their eyes. But I can share with them about the wreckage that I think is appropriate for them to hear developmentally. I don't want them to have a life like I did. My drinking and using kept me from doing things until much later in my life, such as completing high school and starting college. It took years to develop a work ethic. I was so busy being high, I missed a lot of opportunities. I tell them I just don't want them to make the same mistakes. From an informational standpoint I operate on an as-needed basis.

Name each of your children and identify any specific areas you believe you may need to discuss with each child.

More Guidelines for Addressing the Past

The following guidelines are recommended for talking about the past:

- Parents agree on what is and is not shared.*
- Each parent speaks for him- or herself.*
- Parent(s) do not take on the role of the victim.
- Parent(s) display signs of recovery.
- Parent(s) are clear that it is not the children's responsibility to fix or take care of the parents' needs. It is very easy for children to become caught in a triangle of choosing sides and then react on behalf of the parent who is perceived to be the victim.*
- Children are not used as confidants.
- Set the tone for the children to know they can talk with you as they feel the need. To say or imply, "We'll talk about this today and never talk about it again" reinforces the shame of talking honestly.
  *Relevant to two-parent families.

Speaking Beyond the Family

It is important that addiction not be a walled secret. In recovery, sharing about your own addiction is one of the most significant boundaries to learn. You need to learn to discriminate with whom, when, and what to share. Denying the facts, or making a point not to talk openly, implies a stigma is still being attached to the addiction and recovery. Your children need permission not to have to keep the secret of your addiction or recovery. This means they too will need to learn how to discriminate with whom, when, and what they share.

The age of your children and your relationship with them are significant indicators for what to share. Other variables such as family values, ethnic identity and values, neighborhood and community identity, and values that impact the issue of stigma and openness about personal problems are factors as well. Most significant is that your recovery need not be a secret and that your children have people with whom they can share honestly.

Most children don't have a great need to share with many people. Young and adolescent-age children just need their home life to be better. Adult-age children, depending on what is happening in their lives, are more apt not to talk about your recovery unless they feel a sense of pride and are disclosing with their closest friends. Most children of any age hesitate to talk openly about their parents' recovery until they have had some time to trust that it is for real.

Children are in a variety of situations in which it would be very appropriate to say something about the addiction in their lives. They frequently meet others who are reacting to an active addiction, or they already have friends who have lived with it. To be able to talk about their own experiences, which now include recovery, can be an act of passing on the hope and possibility of recovery to others. To be able to be honest about why their family or parents may not attend certain events, or may not stay as long as other families at an event, relieves unnecessary stress. One of the greatest gifts of children being able to talk honestly and openly is that they are often in spontaneous situations where they educate others in a way that continues to lessen the stigma around addiction.

Myra, sixteen, often drives her mother's car to do errands. In her mother's enthusiasm for her recovery, she has two stickers on her car bumper that are reflective of Twelve Step recovery. But those not in Twelve Step programs don't really know what they mean. Myra says she often finds herself explaining to friends and even adults what "First Things First" and "Live and Let Live" mean and how they are relevant in both her and her family's life.

It is from the voices of children that our greatest words of wisdom are spoken. They say things simply and to the point. They may sum up their perception as "My mom is an addict, an alcoholic," or "My mom has a problem with an addiction," or "My dad had a problem and couldn't stop on his own, so he got help and now things are better." If they feel the need to say something, that need is often met with just a few words.

Clifton's father is five years clean and sober, after having spent time in prison for driving under the influence and severely injuring another person in an accident. Clifton's class is required to attend a school event focused on drinking and driving. At the event there is a panel of young people who have been picked up for drinking and driving, and one of the panelists has seriously injured a person. Many students are outraged that a driver could continue to drink after having hurt someone while under the influence.

Clifton isn't comfortable speaking up in the auditorium, but back in the classroom he acknowledges that he knows someone in that position as the driver, and that many times people drink after really negative consequences because they are addicted. He doesn't elaborate; he just makes a statement, not as an adult would, but as a peer with confidence about what he is saying. Clifton does not condone the driver's behavior; he simply states that until the person gets help for the addiction, he most likely will continue to drink and drive. Clifton is planting a seed. He is not responsible for convincing anyone of anything, but the more we have spontaneous ambassadors dropping educational seeds, the more people may garner important information.

Recovering involves both taking action and having faith. Modeling recovery does make a difference to children.

Chapter 7

Creating Healthy Family Traditions

Four generations of my family have experienced the effects of booze. The 1950s were years when my mother drank in front of me. It has taken this long for me to finally be able to tell stories about it without feeling bad. But first I had to go through my own troubled times. In the mid-1970s, my drinking was usually expected since my clients and those around me drank. I had a lot of fun before it turned on me. In the late 1980s and 1990s, the effects of my drinking took a toll on my children and stepchildren. Now that I am older and wiser, I cannot stand to think about alcohol use by my grandkids and the resulting effect. —Gary

Several years ago, country music singer Hank Williams Jr. wrote a song called *Family Tradition* that reflects the effects of a hard-drinking lifestyle upon multigenerations. He talks about getting stoned and singing all night as a family tradition. While many listeners find humor in the lyrics of this song, readers of this book take the words to heart. Unhealthy family traditions, genetics, and the environment contribute to risk factors. Yet there are many things one can do to offer some protection to compensate for the risk.

Research has demonstrated that exposure to a significant number of risk factors in a child's life does not necessarily mean that substance abuse or other problematic behaviors will inevitably follow.[1] The reason for this, according to many researchers, is the presence of protective factors in young people's lives. These protective factors balance and buffer risk factors.[2] This chapter focuses on assisting parents in developing stronger family protective factors.

Risk Factors

Not every child growing up in a family with one or several of the following risk factors becomes an alcoholic or drug abuser, but these factors may increase the likelihood of abuse.[3] Risk factors within the family include

- Unclear expectations of behavior. Children are not given clear messages about what behavior is expected from them.
- Poor monitoring of behavior. Insufficient attention is given to a child's behavior.
- Few and inconsistent rewards of behavior. A child's good behavior is not acknowledged.
- Inconsistent discipline. Parents are very harsh in one situation and lenient in a similar instance.
- Overinvolvement or underinvolvement with children. One parent may be overinvolved with the children while the other is very distant.
- Lack of bonding or closeness between family members. Children may not trust their family members as a source of warmth and support.
- Family conflict. There is conflict between parents and other family members.
- Lack of involvement in family activities. Children are not invited to participate in family tasks, decisions, and activities.
- Family history of alcohol and other drug abuse. One or both parents have a history of alcoholism or other drug abuse, increasing the risk of their children becoming alcoholics or drug addicts, either through environmental exposure or family genetics.
- Condoning alcohol and other drug abuse. Parents or other adults drink, smoke, or abuse substances, setting an example for the children. The risk is further increased if the parents involve children in the behavior, such as by asking a child to get a beer from the refrigerator.

Protective Factors

There are many factors that can protect children, and while these factors are not assurances, they will buffer the risk. The individual and environmental characteristics that contribute to resiliency are called protective factors. It is important to know that the presence of protective factors in the lives of children is more powerful than the presence of risk factors, stresses, or trauma. Resiliency occurs because children develop internal qualities that facilitate this recovery. It also occurs because of support in the children's environment that helps to deflect the impact of the negative.

Parents and others must work to foster internal protective factors in kids, as well as provide environmental protection. The more protective factors present in the life of an individual child, the better it is for the child. However, some researchers are saying that in many cases just a few internal characteristics and environmental supports are enough to shift the balance from risk to resiliency.[4]

The presence of protective factors in the lives of children is more powerful than the presence of risk factors, stresses, or trauma.

Protective factors that can act as a buffer against risk factors[5] include

- close family relationships, where family members are nurturing and supportive of each other
- consistent parenting
- consistent praise, low criticism
- clear expectations, high expectations
- spending quality time with family members
- sharing family responsibilities, including chores and decision making
- coping with stress in positive ways
- encouraging supportive relationships with caring adults beyond the immediate family
- strong bonds with prosocial institutions such as school, community, and church

Both risk and protective factors show consistency across race and cultures.[6]

More risk = increased possibility of behavioral problems
More protective factors = less risk and fewer behavioral
problems

A fifteen-year-old student once said, "Resiliency means bouncing back from problems and stuff with more power and smarts than you started with."

Children within a family will differ in their resiliency as a result of the fact that they came into the family system at a different time, which often means there were different influences. Dina, whom we have followed in this book, recognizes her older children have been subject to much more family upheaval and chaos than her younger children. She clearly sees that the older two have risk factors her younger children do not have, such as inconsistent discipline, lack of involvement, and poor monitoring of their activities. Her younger children also have more protective factors than the older two; they have more outside activities that they find pride in, and they have a stronger connection to their friends' parents.

Resiliency researchers have documented that just one key adult[7] in a child's life who helps that child feel special and of value can make a difference. More than anything, children need the chance to bond with adults who are meaningful and important to them.

Dillon's children identified significant adults in their lives; his daughter talked about two of her friends' mothers who had extended themselves to her in loving ways; his son talked about a coach at school who made him feel he was talented and likeable.

Most adults who make a difference in a child's life, and who impart to a child that he or she has worth, are members of the extended family, such as aunts, uncles, grandparents, a friend's parent, or a teacher at school. There are many other possibilities, but when young or adult children are asked which adults somehow let them know they were of value, had worth, and were liked, these are their most common answers.

A Word of Caution

Out of fear and wanting some reassurances, it is typical for parents to immediately add up the risk factors and compare them to the protective factors. While this may offer some comfort, it is unlikely to give a clear picture of the influences in a child's life.

It is easy for the addicted parent to go into denial and say, "Well, it wasn't that bad. I was alcoholic but their mother compensated for a lot of my behavior." Or, "I was still there as a parent a lot of the time." The reality is, the nonaddicted parent can only compensate so much, and he or she may not have compensated as much as you think. It is very likely he or she became codependent; focused on enabling you; succumbed to depression, anxiety, or exhaustion; or possibly displayed rageful behavior. There may have been enmeshment, where a parent makes the child a confidant. By being an addict, you have affected your children by your behavior.

So while it can be helpful to you, the recovering parent, to know what may have influenced your children negatively or positively, the place to focus your parental attention is on identifying, reinforcing, and expanding upon the protective factors already present in your children's environment. Couple this identification with the message "What is right with me is more powerful than anything wrong." What is most important now is to begin to offer more constructive parenting. None of us can change the past, but we can learn from it, accept it, and move on, focusing on new possibilities that come with each day.

A Functioning Family

The following are five areas of family functioning that will support you in creating resilient children, and to some degree can be applied to your adult-age children as well.

1. affection, support, and affirmation
2. communication
3. maintaining a positive family identity
4. problem solving
5. providing physical safety

Affection, Support, and Affirmation

Many parents are scared silly at the thought of how to parent their children, often not knowing how to get close to their kids.

Parenting really starts with listening. Listen to your children and facilitate their desires. For example, you are going to a movie; let them choose. Look for the humor, the excitement, or the positive in the movie. Try to see the movie through their eyes. Foster your children's interests, not just what you want them to be interested in. Explore various opportunities and activities with your child and then be there to watch and encourage.

Children of all ages need parents to sing their praises.

Children of all ages need their parents to applaud them for just being and to give them feedback about what they like about them. Parents need to be specific with children about the characteristics they value in them, such as their humor, their creativity, and their thoughtfulness. Unfortunately, for some children, the only validation they may receive is in taking care of another family member, staying out of sight, or being part of "image management" for the family to look good and bring validation to the family.

Identify five traits or qualities you respect and admire about each of your children. Try to focus more on who they are rather than on what they have done.

For example, you may say, "I am proud of my son for being a good ball player." What is it about him that makes him a good ball player? Is it his sense of dedication, his willingness to be a team player, his self-discipline? Or you may say, "I am so happy my daughter is a good actress." What is it about her that makes her such a good actress? Is it her creativity? Is it her ability to listen to others and be empathetic to them?

List five qualities you respect and admire about each of your children.

Name _____	Name _____	Name _____
1.	1.	1.
2.	2.	2.
3.	3.	3.
4.	4.	4.
5.	5.	5.

The challenge of unconditional love is in not just showing it when your kids get good grades, when their rooms are clean, or when they bring the car back on time, but in being able to show unconditional love when none of the above is true. Do not confuse the idea of loving your children with loving how your children behave. Now is the opportunity to distinguish between their worth and their behavior. While the behavior may not be lovable, the child is.

Name each of your children and answer the following questions:
    In the past week, have you told each of your children who live in the home what it is you appreciate or love about them?

For the children who do not live in the home, young or adult, have you told them recently what it is you appreciate or love about them?

If your answer is no, is this something you are willing to do now?

If not, what is getting in the way? If you have a problem expressing love and appreciation, talk to a trusted friend, a counselor, or a sponsor.

When you begin this practice and it seems to flow, you can do this on a daily basis.

List six ways you demonstrate love toward your children.
1.
2.
3
4.
5.
6.

Which of these behaviors have you demonstrated in the past twenty-four hours?

Which of these behaviors have you demonstrated in the past week?

If you have not demonstrated such behavior within a week, this should be a wake-up call or bell ringer.

If your children are not living at home:

Which of these behaviors have you demonstrated within the last month?

Which of these behaviors have you demonstrated within the last six months?

Which of these behaviors do your children appreciate?

What are some other ways that you could demonstrate your love for them?

Children need to hear you say "I love you." You are trying to say that in your behavior, but they need to hear the words as well. If saying "I love you" is difficult, it is my hope you will learn to say it with ease, and in time come to be able to say it often.

Say "I love you," and say it often. Remember, "I love you" is a complete sentence.

When people have difficulty sharing intimately, they often create excuses such as, "Oh, I am sure I've told her I love her. Why do I need to say it again?" Saying "I love you" validates your children for their very presence and creates intimacy between you and them. Saying "I love you" is not the same as having loving feelings or doing loving things for your children. Children need to experience love in many ways, including being told. Tell them because you want to, because it is what you are feeling, period. Avoid connecting it to something your child has done. "I love you" is a complete sentence. If it is difficult to say, write it down and leave it under your child's pillow, under a magnet on the refrigerator door, or in a book he or she is reading. Be creative and enjoy the process. There are also other ways to impart this endearing message. As you say good-bye in a telephone conversation, include "I love you." When you drop your child off at school or work, say "love you." Or when your child goes to bed, it can be a part of saying good night.

You must also be empathetic to the child who has heard these words so many times and wasn't able to trust your sincerity. In a treatment program, a father sitting across from his fifteen-year-old son said, "I love you, Derrick." Derrick looked at his father and simply said, "Don't tell me that anymore; show me." That is hard for a parent to hear, but this young boy had heard the "I love you" before. He heard these words when his father was loaded, and after his father had been absent for days, and now in treatment. He interpreted these words as a way of saying, "Don't be angry with me." He felt his father was not being sincere, and not really thinking about Derrick. Words have little meaning compared to behavior, and his father's sobriety is what is needed at this time. So if "I love you" was freely expressed but associated with being under the influence, this is an area where your child may need more time so that he or she can trust those words.

Some recovering parents genuinely feel that their children are strangers. "How can I say I love my child when I don't even know my child?" "I don't know my child because I was too out of it in my addiction." Or, "I wasn't even in my child's life." Jason's father, now that he is sober, feels a fatherly responsibility to be accountable to his son. He has other children from previous marriages and has never been accountable to them. At this time his other children want nothing to do with him, but Jason does. His father is quick to say, "I don't know if it is love I feel, or just some responsibility. Whatever, it would be good for me, and most likely good for my son, to have a sober and loving environment in which to live." Now that is a lot of honesty, and Jason's father is not the first to feel this way. If Jason's dad takes the time to be with his son, and to look for common interests, his son will likely come to feel the love, but it will have a lot to do with his recovery.

In recovery it is very likely you will come to like yourself better and be able to receive love and care from others. You will find ways to extend yourself to others in a caring manner. Much of what you learn from your peers you can apply to your child who seems to be a stranger today.

 Name each of your children and then answer the following questions for each child.

What facts do you know about your children? (Grade in school, major in school, what they do in their work, who their friends are, whether or not they have boyfriend or girlfriend.)

What would be helpful to know?

What are their likes or dislikes?
What do they like to eat?
What music do they like?
Do they like to be outdoors or indoors?
What do they like in people?
Who are their closest friends?
What have they been challenged with in life? Be aware that you have probably been one of their greater challenges, but other challenges could be school, friends, possibly a health issue.

Expressing love and caring does not come naturally for many of us, but it can be a natural result of new recovery behaviors. The more recovering people "show up" for loved ones, the easier it becomes to be in touch with hurts and joys of family members. Pat shared:

I can remember hugging my twenty-two-year-old son, maybe for the first time. I was close to being sober for nine months. For so many years he had wanted to be close to me and I never had time for him. One night I happened to stop by his house and he was crying; his girlfriend had just broken up with him. I didn't know what to say, but suddenly I just walked over to him and hugged him. I really held him. We both cried. I couldn't believe it. I hadn't hugged anyone in a long time and I didn't like all the hugging I saw when I first got sober. Then I came to like it, and then I began to give hugs, and suddenly that was the turning point for my son and me.

Communication
Parents communicate with their children to teach, guide, console, achieve closeness, and plan and accomplish the practical necessities of life. Capable parents regulate what they say and how they speak to their children. Conversations are clear, flexible, open, and responsive. In the past, it is possible that your children have experienced your communication as curt and withholding, or you spoke with no regard for being understood or for understanding anyone else. You may have given out too much information. Communication was more likely to have been lecturing, blaming, dismissing, and often shaming. As a consequence your children may not have learned to ask for their needs to be met, or they just took what they could, or went without.

An adult son of an addict said, "My father would come home from work, eat alone, go to his computer, where he would spend the evening, and then go to bed. I have heard some people describe my father as a quiet man, but really he was a rejecting man. My brothers, sisters, and I were all subject to his punishing silence, his silent rage."

James described his communication with his children as being limited to only when he wanted to say something. He doesn't remember being genuinely interested in listening to his kids from the time they were very young, and he knows there were times he belittled them and was blaming toward them. Dillon says he was a lecturer to his children with no regard for what any one of them said. Dina said she basically pleaded and whined with her kids just to get them to do things.

These types of communication tell children that they are not worth talking to and are of little value. Healthy communication is about listening with honor and speaking with respect, as the following story by Greg illustrates:

I am applying my recovery directly to my relationships with my two children. I have always tried to control my kids, even from a distance. I controlled how they spent their time and what they wanted for themselves. Today I don't do that. Today I really listen to them. Something incredible happens when I listen. In the act of listening, I am empowering them and they are learning. It is great. They are not learning just because they can now make their own mistakes; they are learning because they are making good choices. It is me who had to change.

Listen to find out who the other person is and what he or she has to say, not to formulate your defense. Maintain healthy boundaries and protect yourself as you listen by determining if what is being said is "true," "not true," or "questionable." If what you hear is true, take in the information without interpreting it as a statement of your worth. Experience your feelings about what you hear. If what you hear is not true, take in the information, acknowledge your feelings about it, then strive to work through your feelings, reminding yourself, "This is not about me." If what you hear is questionable, ask for the information you need in order to decide if it is true or not true. Ask for this information without complaining, blaming, or explaining why you need it.

When blaming, preaching, or lecturing, sentences invariably begin with "You . . ." Simple, yet not-so-easy steps to better communication are "I" statements. "I saw . . . ," "I felt . . . ," "I thought . . . ," "I heard . . ." Remind yourself you are speaking to be known. It is interesting to note that when speaking from a position of "I," it automatically shortens your verbal discourse, which is usually quite helpful in being heard as well. If you find you can't speak from the "I," you may want to say nothing until you can.

Here are some examples of ways to rephrase your communication from "you" statements to "I" statements. Instead of saying, "You always come home late," you could say, "I get worried when you don't call to say you're running late." Instead of saying, "You never do your chores," you could say, "I feel overwhelmed when I have to do all the housework."

Maintaining a Positive Family Identity
The foundation of a healthy family identity is a shared feeling of pride and kinship. Parents and children share the following beliefs:

- Home is a safe, welcoming place.
- We have a past that is a source of strength.
- We like each other.
- We trust each other.
- We enrich each other's joys and support one another in times of sorrow.
- We can communicate with each other.

Children raised with addiction often see themselves as alone and are often physically separate from the adults in the family. These children may feel isolated and crushed when their parents mishandle celebrations. For some, family gatherings merely intensify each other's misery. Family traditions and rituals are not about feelings of pride and may involve alcohol or drugs. Celebrations are often cold and meaningless, angry or chaotic, or overlooked and ignored.

Healthy, functioning families take deliberate steps to cultivate and pass on a positive identity to the children. Healthy families keep traditions and form family rituals. Children in such families see themselves as part of a unit larger than themselves and take pleasure in belonging.

What are the traditions or rituals in your family?
What is the focus of these rituals?
What do they say to your children?
What feelings do they evoke?
Review what you and your family do for birthdays. Is each child acknowledged on his or her birthday? In what manner? Are special birthdays singled out for added celebration, such as becoming a teenager or an adult? Is this something to which you would like to give greater consideration?

Do you have daily family rituals, such as in the morning? After school? At dinnertime? At bedtime? Children growing up with addiction often describe family members just heading out in different directions in the morning, after school, and maybe even at dinner. As one young girl said, "We took our food from the stove and each went quickly to our own rooms or to the television set. At bedtime, we each just disappeared."

When healthy rituals have been nonexistent, they usually need to be created slowly with input from the kids. You could use the idea of creating rituals, particularly around a holiday or birthday celebration, as a topic for a family meeting. In the case of individual birthdays, you could ask each child what he or she would like that would help create feelings of being special. It will take time for certain rituals to evolve, and you may want to try out different things. Just let your children know you want to do it differently. Don't try to change everything immediately. In the early years of recovery be open to this, gradually building from year to year.

If mealtimes have been disruptive, painful, or simply a time of non-connection and you want to create change, start with the mealtime that is most likely to be easier to establish a better connection with each other.

Recently a recovering mother told me that her twenty-one-year-old and twenty-four-year-old sons told her one of the best things she and her husband did was insist that they eat breakfast together each morning. In this case, breakfast was simple. Everyone put together their own meal, but they all sat at the table at the same time to begin the day.

Eating dinner with your children six or seven nights a week and turning off the television during dinner substantially reduces the risk of children smoking, drinking, and using drugs.[8]

If your family is becoming closer already, what could be incorporated that would bring greater harmony or closeness? It could be simple changes, such as everyone sitting down and beginning the meal by stating one positive thing that happened during the day. Or with the family holding hands around the table and sharing a moment of silence. You could have a weekly ritual where everyone takes part in cooking the meal. Be creative and get input from others. But take it slowly and keep it simple. These types of changes can seem like you have just landed from outer space.

Ask your family members what types of family traditions they have liked. They may recognize some rituals and parts of rituals that you haven't. This is a great time to involve the children in creating new rituals. This does not need to be elaborate; a bedtime ritual may be as simple as acknowledging your children when they go to bed. Or, getting up with them in the morning, ensuring they get something to eat. Or, once a week stopping for ice cream on the way home from school.

A new holiday ritual could involve the family doing community service work together, such as working at a food shelter. A Christmas ritual could be everyone going to choose the tree together. Including your children in creating a different celebration of a holiday, birthday, or family ritual is an opportunity for powerful family healing.

Don't forget, your being clean and sober is the greatest beginning of any and all healthy family traditions and rituals.

Problem Solving

Everyone encounters problems. What's important is how you handle your problems. Healthy families use constructive strategies for solving problems. Troubled or addictive families are "knocked out" by their problems and give children the idea that life will easily defeat them or often ignore them.

Michael grew up with dyslexia, and it was a source of shame for his parents and himself. They only spoke of it behind closed doors and did not want others to know. They associated Michael's problem with being defective, or not being as smart as others. Michael struggled through much of his early years of school, but in high school he was befriended by his English and math teachers, who took it upon themselves to get an appropriate diagnosis for Michael. Michael was sent to special classes to help him learn to read, and ironically, he went on to become a physician. When his own son displayed signs of struggling with school classes, Michael deliberately sought out a different manner in which to cope. He had the ability to allow a problem to be just that, a problem, not a crisis.

Members of families with addictions often have either learned to minimize to such an extent they don't see a problem until it reaches crisis proportions, or they don't take action, allowing a problem to simmer until a crisis occurs. When there is a problem, family members often blame or adopt a victim stance. Try to remain neutral. Most daily problems will be worked through within a short period of time and often won't even be remembered.

Healthy families problem solve by

- defining the difficulty
- accepting that problems are a normal part of life and not a stigma, punishment, or sign of weakness
- working together to find a solution
- assigning a leadership role to parents while allowing other family members to express their views

Resilient children learn problem-solving skills by observing and being allowed the opportunity to be a part of handling problems and performing tasks. However, children need to be able to learn the appropriate skills to do so. Opportunity without skill leads to frustration and failure. At home, children can play a role in managing family life by doing chores, taking care of a pet, or helping to plan vacations. The family can take concrete steps to help a child develop competency in whatever the task, from baking a cake from a mix, to feeding the animals, to helping a parent do mechanical work on a car.

If your children are adults, they already may be modeling "crisis" mentality—every problem is a crisis. They may be modeling defeat with every difficulty. If your relationship is such that you know they are having difficulty, you can possibly model new skills that you are learning. Help to define the difficulty. Don't perceive the difficulty as punishment or a sign of weakness, and identify whether or not more information is needed to accurately assess the crisis. Emotionally detach yourself, and you can even change the terminology to diminish the perceived intensity of the crisis—a dilemma, a problem, or a situation. Gather data, identify possibilities, and make choices.

When a problem arises, gather data, identify possibilities, and make choices.

Providing Physical Safety

Physical safety is the family's primary obligation. Are the basic physical needs of your children (shelter, food, clothing) being taken care of? If you are a divorced parent, are you paying child support? Do you owe back support? If you cannot pay the full amount, pay something, and work with the child support office to problem solve how you can be more accountable.

If there has been physical abuse or raging behavior, anger management classes may be necessary. If you have worked with a counselor or therapist, that professional may be a resource to assist you in locating such a class. Your county mental health services are another resource.

If you have been physically abusive in the past, it is possible the physical abuse will continue, even in recovery. You and your family need to work with a counselor who specializes in domestic violence. If you are still engaging in abuse and there are children in the home, for the sake of their safety I encourage you to call the local authorities. As difficult as this may be, hospital emergency rooms, state and county social service agencies, and local sheriff and police departments will be able to make a referral so that you can get the help you need.

If sexual abuse has occurred, it is paramount that you call a local social service agency to get the appropriate treatment for both the victim and perpetrator. It is very likely that even with recovery the abuse will continue. Even if the abuse does not continue, the victim needs specialized assistance to cope with what has occurred. If the addicted parent is the offender, it is faulty thinking to assume the sexual abuse will not recur just because of recovery from the addiction.

Reshaping Family Roles

In the early years of understanding children from alcoholic families, it was extremely helpful for people to identify their own role in the context of the family. The concept of family roles became important because it offered a framework that helped affected families understand what was happening in their lives. Defining and explaining the roles has helped people to understand why it took so long for their pain to begin to show. To know more about roles, I suggest reading two of my earlier books, *It Will Never Happen to Me* and *Changing Course*.

The roles that children assume become roles of survivorship in which they develop useful skills, but due to being fueled by fear and the rigidity with which someone holds on to their roles, there are corresponding skill deficits. Should you see your children in particular roles, the following information will offer suggestions to reinforce additional behaviors that will allow them to maintain the skill of their roles and learn new skills that will offer greater emotional maturity.

While this is most effective with younger and adolescent-age children, there are some behaviors and messages you can reinforce with your adult-age children depending on how frequently you see them.

The Responsible Child, the Hero
The responsible child is the little adult, taking responsibility for him- or herself and others in the family. Such responsible children demonstrate initiative, leadership skills, and decision-making skills, but they often become perfectionists, are less likely to learn teamwork, have difficulty listening, and have a strong need to be in control.

Recommended parental behaviors:

- Give attention to the child at times when he or she is not achieving.
- Validate the child's intrinsic worth, and try to separate his or her feelings of self-worth from achievements.
- Let the child know it's okay to make a mistake.
- Emphasize parts of the child's character not yet actualized: his or her playfulness, spontaneity, ability to rely on someone else.
- Praise the child at times when he or she is not necessarily in a leader role, such as when on a team but not the captain.
- Reinforce that you will be responsible; he or she can be the child.

The Acting-out Child, the Rebel or Scapegoat
The acting-out child is the angry, rebellious child. Typically these children are the voices crying out for help. While other children in the family draw positive attention (hero), or no attention (adjuster), the acting-out child contributes to the severity of his or her own situation by eliciting the kind of attention that causes parents to cry, nag, and belittle the child.

Recommended parental behaviors:

- Give the child compliments and encouragement whenever he or she takes responsibility for something.
- Attempt to develop empathy for the child.
- Set limits. Give clear explanations of the child's responsibilities and clear choices and consequences.
- Let the child know when his or her behavior is inappropriate.

The Adjusting Child, the Invisible One
The adjusting child is often lost in the shuffle. This child has become adept at being flexible and has found the best way to survive is not to draw attention to self. The adjusting child does not learn how to take the lead or show initiative and has difficulty perceiving choices and options that could be available.

Recommended parental behaviors:

- Point out and encourage the child's strengths, talents, and creativity.
- Engage in one-to-one contact to learn more about the individual child.
- Bring the child into decision-making processes, giving him or her win-win choices.
- Try to pick up on the child's personal interests.

The Clown, the Mischief Maker
The clown is funny or distracting and gets attention frequently. This child likes to hide, make faces, pull the chair out from under someone else, stick chalk in the erasers, and otherwise act out. This child is a wonderful distracter from the family pain, but has difficulty staying present and focused

when needed, and doesn't know appropriate ways in which to ask for attention or get his or her needs met.

Recommended parental behaviors:

- Give the child responsibilities with some importance.
- Hold the child accountable.
- Encourage responsible behavior.
- Encourage appropriate sense of humor.
- Insist on eye contact.

The Placater, the Caretaker

The placater is often referred to as the household social worker, and he or she tends to focus on helping other people to feel better. This person's job is to lessen the family pain. Placaters are quite empathetic, compassionate, and great listeners, but they are very separated from what they need or want. They develop a high tolerance for inappropriate behavior and have few self-protective boundaries.

Recommended parental behaviors:

- Assist the child in focusing on him- or herself, instead of others.
- Help this child play.
- When the child is assisting another, ask the child to identify what he or she is feeling.
- Validate the child's intrinsic worth, separating worth from his or her caretaking.
- Reinforce that you will take care of yourself and other family members.

Deepening and Mending Relationships

Family Time

Making time for your children is one of the most important parenting acts you need to do. Depending on the availability of everyone's schedule, it is highly recommended that the entire family engage in a family activity at least once a week. If that is not feasible, then make it every two weeks. In early recovery you may be very busy with many meetings, but if your family is a priority, then you need to create space and time for family activities.

If finances are a consideration, organize a family barbecue, play a family-focused game, watch a video and eat popcorn together, or take a hike. If one child is a part of a school event, such as a school play or debate, the family activity might be as simple as eating together, then traveling and sitting together at the event. What is important is that it be an activity involving the entire family and not interrupted by others. You want your family to heal, and healing occurs by giving them your time.

You want your family to heal, and healing occurs by giving them your time.

Individual Time

It is also important that each parent have his or her special time with each child during the week. This time may be a dinner, a movie, playing a game or sports activity, or it can be a ride to the yogurt shop. Make a list with your child of possible activities the two of you could do together that are doable in a short amount of time, maybe just a half hour a week. Then let your child choose. What is most important is consistency and that your child knows this date is a priority and your time will be solely devoted to him or her.

Family Meetings

Family meetings can be wonderful rituals that facilitate an opportunity for support and affirmation, healthy communication, family connection, and problem solving. If such meetings are introduced in the process of gradual change in a newly recovering family, or if you and your family have experienced family treatment and family meetings were introduced there, they are more likely to be successful. To announce that the family will now have family meetings because you are a few weeks clean and sober is not necessarily going to get a warm reception. Think about how you want to introduce the concept and get your family's thoughts about such a meeting.

Family meetings can occur with children of any age. Many recovering families will even have meetings with their adult children who no longer live at home. While face-to-face meetings are the best, families living at great distances might have a conference call on the telephone or use instant messaging on the Internet.

If families like this idea, most families still raising children choose to have it weekly. It is always possible to have a nightly mini-version. If the children are independent and living away from home, it may be more realistic to meet monthly. First and foremost, the frequency, the time of day, and the location must be workable. A family meeting itself would be a great place to make these decisions with everyone's input.

A "sacred" time and place for family meetings needs to be agreed upon by all family members. Be realistic about the amount of time needed. Once agreed upon, it is essential that the sacred time be honored above any other activity or event. Keeping a sacred time for the family meeting demonstrates the fact that the family members see the family as more important than anything, so cell phones, television, radio, and pagers need to be turned off. Any outside intrusion needs to be guarded against.

Ground rules help. Everyone gets a chance to talk; one person talks at a time without interruption. Everyone listens, and only positive, constructive feedback is allowed. Each meeting begins with a different person. If a child is resistant, you can offer incentives such as a post-meeting pizza or a special position for the week, such as rule enforcer.

You could also establish that any family member can request a family meeting to address a particular issue. Such meetings may only be minutes in length; nonetheless, the time is honored as "family meeting time," which means all family members come together to listen in the spirit of cooperation.

Some possible agendas for family meetings are discussions on feelings, dealing with family business, and giving affirmations.

- *Feelings.* Everyone shares the feelings they have experienced this week. What feelings have I had that I talked about? What feelings have I had that I haven't talked about? Feelings don't have to be specific to family relationships but should be the predominant focus. If someone is having feelings about something important that occurred outside the family, it is still relevant that the person sees the family as a place in which to share, be heard, and be supported. In a feelings meeting, the agenda is not to problem solve feelings (unless the speaker asks for assistance in problem solving); the goal is to share and be heard. If someone asks for assistance in problem solving, continue through the group so that all have shared feelings and then go around a second time for problem solving.

- *Family Business.* Everyone contributes to problem solving any issues concerning household tasks, such as who is feeding the pets and mowing the lawn, or issues around money, such as allowances, summer jobs, cars, and insurance. Family business might have to do with coping with a family stressor, such as the absence of a family member or an illness. Perhaps it will be a meeting at which each person presents a situation for input and problem solving. It could be a current problem, or it could be a situation that has occurred in the past week and has already been handled, but having input for a future situation would be helpful. It could be an individual problem outside the family, or it could involve members of the family.

- *Affirmation.* In every meeting there is the possibility for affirmation of self and others. You might begin each meeting by having family members share what they did this week that was good for them or that supported their recovery. A young child might say, "I asked a question in class," when in the past he or she would have wondered about something and not asked. A teenager might say, "I didn't go out with a group of kids that I knew were going to get into some trouble," or "I called home and asked to be picked up when I was with some friends and they began to smoke dope." A mother might say, "I allowed you to cry without trying to stop you," when in the past she would have tried to convince her daughter she didn't need to feel bad. A father might say, "I am making a point to leave work early so that I get home in time for dinner."

A fun way to conclude a family meeting is with affirmations of self. Family members say something positive about themselves and, once said, the family cites back, "Yes, you are!"

"I am a fun person to be with."	"Yes, you are!"
"I am a loving person."	"Yes, you are!"
"I am worthy."	"Yes, you are!"

As you are creating changes in your family, remember there is no such thing as a perfect parent. Healthy parenting doesn't occur overnight just because recovery has begun. You need to feel good about the healthy parenting that occurred in spite of your addiction and know that today, in recovery, you have the opportunity to make choices to be an even better parent.

Chapter 8

Never Underestimate Your Power as a Parent

As a parent, I talk to my kids about peer pressure and the fact that they don't need to surrender to it. I tell them they need to be careful about making a decision they may regret. I state clearly that they are not to smoke cigarettes, drink, smoke dope, or use any drugs. I tell them once they smoke a cigarette they might not be able to go back, so don't start. I tell them when they are much older they will have choices, but today they can't afford to make a choice they might not be able to take back. My big message is don't make bad choices. I am aware of where they are, what they are doing, and who they are with. —Becky

You may hear yourself saying things like, "Given my history, what can I possibly say to my children? They will just see me as a hypocrite!" Let go of that thinking immediately. Who better than you, a recovering parent, to talk to your children? All parents struggle with "Do as I say, not as I do." You are fortunate to be able to put it in the past tense, "Do as I say, not as I did." It is quite likely you will hear, "But you did it," from one of your teenagers or adult children. Younger children may not have witnessed your drinking or drug use so it is not as real for them. They have also had fewer years in which to become angry with you and to use that anger to avoid listening.

If your older children toss the hypocrite line at you, spare yourself any self-flagellation; you don't need to accept it. Your job is to parent effectively, and that is what you intend to do.

Here are two points that may support you in talking to your children:

1. Children do listen to their parents about important issues.[1]
2. Pervasive, consistent messages to young people about drugs and alcohol have a strong influence in preventing substance abuse.[2]

Research has shown that a significant key to preventing substance disorders is to delay the onset of alcohol and drug use. For each year adolescents delay the use of alcohol, they decrease the odds of lifelong dependence by 14 percent and lifelong abuse by 8 percent.[3] The results are similar for drugs. Studies show reductions of 5 percent for lifelong dependence and 4 percent for lifelong abuse for every year adolescents delay initial use.[4]

Messages to Children about Use of Alcohol and Drugs

Realistically, most children at some point in their lives will choose to drink alcohol, and some will try other drugs. However, the repetition of strong nonuse messages that you give to your children will have a delaying effect for onset of use. There are other protective factors as well, especially proactive parenting and strong family bonds. These can help delay adolescent experimentation with drugs and alcohol and thus help reduce long-term problems.

Parents must talk to their children about alcohol and drug abuse when they are young and continue to talk about it often. Kids do listen to their parents about important issues in their lives.

Preschoolers
It may seem premature to talk about alcohol and drugs with children who have not yet started school, but attitudes and habits formed at this young age can have an important bearing on the decisions they will make when they are older. Preschoolers are eager to know and memorize rules, and they want your opinion of what is bad and what is good. They are old enough to grasp the fact that certain things are bad for them.

- Limit the fast foods in your children's diet. Offer healthy, nutritious food and discuss with your children why you eat this way. Have your children name several favorite healthy foods and explain how these foods contribute to health and strength. Introduce the concept of unhealthy foods, such as those consisting predominantly of sugar or fat.

- Set aside regular times when you can give your young children your full attention. Play with them; let them know you love them; tell them they are too wonderful and unique to do drugs or alcohol.
- Provide guidelines for your children, such as playing fair, sharing toys, and telling the truth so they know what kind of behavior you expect from them. This sets the stage for future dialogue regarding expectations.
- Encourage your children to follow instructions and to ask questions if they do not understand the instructions. This encourages your children to benefit from the wisdom of adults and be able to ask questions to garner a greater understanding.
- Strengthen your children's problem-solving skills by giving them the opportunity and the skills to strategize problem solving and not feel defeated and frustrated. This will offer your children healthy ways to feel empowerment and control.
- Point out poisonous and harmful substances commonly found in homes, such as bleach, furniture polish, and insect repellent. Read the products' warning labels out loud to your children. Explain that not all bad substances have warnings on them, so they should only eat food or take medicine that a trusted person gives them.

Children Ages 5–8

At this age your children are showing an increased interest in the world outside the family and home. Now is the time to explain to them that some people use alcohol and drugs even though they are harmful, and sometimes people start using a drug just to see what it feels like, but it turns into an addiction. Young children can understand the concept of addiction—that alcohol or drug use can become a very bad habit and it is difficult to stop. Tell your children that even a small amount of alcohol can make them sick as alcohol has a much greater negative effect on a child's brain and body than on an adult's brain and body. Explain how alcohol and drugs interfere with the way our bodies work and how we think, and can make a person very sick or even cause them to die. Praise your children for taking good care of their bodies and avoiding things that might hurt them.

By the time your children are ready to enter fourth grade, they should have an understanding of

- how foods, poisons, and medicines differ from illegal drugs and alcohol
- how medicines prescribed by a doctor and administered by a responsible adult may help during an illness but can be very harmful if misused
- how alcohol and drugs are harmful to children's developing brains and bodies

Here's how one recovering father addressed the difference between illegal drugs and doctor-prescribed medication. "I tell my kids that all things on this earth have functions, but when we misuse and abuse them, they become hurtful. My younger child has to take medication, so I explain to him that many drugs are helpful but other ones are not. I let him know that the drug he uses is very helpful and that it is different from the drugs his mother and I once used."

> **Two-thirds of fourth graders polled said that they wished their parents would talk more with them about drugs.**[5]

Children Ages 9–11

As children move up in elementary school or enter intermediate school, friends become extremely important, and peers and older children will often expose them to alcohol and drugs. It is vital that your children's anti-alcohol and antidrug attitudes be strong, as the earlier children begin using these substances, the more likely they are to experience serious problems.

At this age children can handle more sophisticated discussions about why people are attracted to drugs. It is likely that you and your children know people whose use of alcohol and/or drugs has caused pain in their lives. Use your children's curiosity about major traumatic events in people's lives, such as a car accident or divorce, to discuss how the abuse of alcohol and drugs can cause these events.

Television and other forms of media from music to videos will bombard children with messages that imply alcohol makes a person popular, happy, and desirable by the opposite sex. You may be thinking, "but she is just a little girl," or "he is just a boy." By fifth and sixth grade, however, children begin to acquire positive expectancies about alcohol, meaning they are identifying what is perceived as the arousing and positive effects of alcohol use. Prior to this age their alcohol expectancies tend to be negative, such as, "Alcohol can make me sick, mean, or argumentative."[6] Include in your discussions with your children how alcohol and tobacco are promoted via advertising, song lyrics, movies, and television, making the use of these substances appear glamorous.

There are opportunities for "teachable moments." These moments may occur when you are walking down the street and see a group of teenagers drinking and hanging out. Or the front page of the newspaper has a story about a young mother who had her child taken away when she was arrested for drug dealing. Whatever the situation may be, these moments are an opportunity for spontaneous conversations, but it requires a willingness on your part to engage around these issues.

Praise your children for thinking for themselves. You can't stand over them and direct them; they need the opportunity to show they can make good choices, so be sure you give them the chance to think for themselves.

Children this age also love to know how things work. This age group can be fascinated by how drugs affect the user's brain and body.

Most importantly, explain that the use of alcohol or other drugs strongly hurts the growth and development of the brain. Drinking alcohol or using drugs can permanently alter the brain. It will not just affect your children's memory and the ability to think and problem solve while they are drinking or using, it can alter those abilities so they are never able to make good decisions and have good judgment for themselves. Explain to your children how anything taken in excess can be dangerous. Younger children are more apt to be impacted by this than older ones; now is the time for these messages.

Before leaving elementary or intermediate school your children should know

- the immediate effects of alcohol and drug use on different parts of the body, including the risks of coma or a fatal overdose
- the long-term consequences of alcohol and drug abuse; how and why drugs can be addicting and how they make people who use them lose control of their lives
- the problems that alcohol and other drugs cause the user, the user's family and friends, and the world

Rehearse with your children possible scenarios in which friends offer them drugs or alcohol. Have your children practice delivering an emphatic, "That stuff is really bad for you!" Give them permission to use you as an excuse. "My mom and dad will kill me if I drink a beer!" Upsetting parents is one of the top reasons preteens give for why they don't use drugs or alcohol.

Children frequently begin to have their early experiences with alcohol, tobacco, and possibly other drugs at ages ten, eleven, and twelve. This is most likely to occur when they are unsupervised in their own home or at the home of friends.

It is essential you know your children's friends, where they hang out, and what they like to do. Equally important, know the parents of your children's friends so you can reinforce each other's efforts and discuss with them general and specific concerns about raising children in a highly addictive society.

Reinforce that you will always verify there will be adult supervision if your child is going to their home and you hope they will do the same. This will put you in closer touch with your children's daily lives, and you will be in a better position to recognize trouble spots.

Children Ages 12–14

While your greatest opportunity to offer influential parenting is with your younger children, never underestimate the influence that could still occur.

Although teens often seem unreceptive to their parents as they struggle to become independent, they need parental protection, support, involvement, and guidance more than ever. Adolescence is a confusing and stressful time, characterized by mood changes and deep insecurity, and teens struggle to figure out who they are and how they fit in while establishing their own identities.

Your teenage children are often experiencing a conflict with their natural urges to seek validation from peers and to solidify their identity with a peer group. If you are in early recovery and suddenly more available to them for the first time in many years, this leaves many children sarcastically saying, "Like, where were you the first ten or twelve years of my life, thank you?"

It is difficult to sort out what is adolescent resistance and what is related to anger about the loss of relationship that came with your addiction, but that is not the issue here. The issue is you have a teenager and you need to show up and be the best parent you can be. One of the most important supports for yourself is to talk to others who have had teenagers, and those presently raising them, to help you not feel so alone and unique in your experiences. As alone as you may feel, there is very little that will be unique in raising a teenager.

At this time in your child's life it is still important that you know where your children are and who they are with.

A child whose friends are drinking and using drugs is very likely to be drinking and using drugs too.[7]

Your child's transition from intermediate or elementary school to middle school or junior high calls for special vigilance as children are more vulnerable to drugs and other risky behaviors when they move up to a new school.

All of the measures listed below are critically important in making sure that your children's lives are structured in such a way that alcohol and drugs have no place to fit in.

- If possible, arrange to have your children looked after and engaged in an activity from 3:00 to 5:00 P.M. Encourage them to get involved with youth groups, art, music, sports, community service, and academic clubs.
- Make sure children who are unattended for any period during the day feel your presence. Give them a schedule and set limits on their behavior. Give them household chores to accomplish. Enforce a strict "phone in to you" policy. Leave notes for them around the house. Provide easy-to-find snacks. Don't allow visitors in the house when there is no adult supervision.
- Set and enforce curfews. Weekend curfews might range from 9:00 P.M. for a child in fifth grade to 12:30 A.M. for a senior in high school. Encourage an open dialogue with your children about their experiences. "I need to know what is going on in your life so I can be a good parent to you. I love you and I trust you, but I don't trust the world and the temptations around you."
- Get to know the parents of your children's friends and exchange

phone numbers and addresses. Have all parents agree to forbid each other's children from consuming alcohol and other drugs in their homes and pledge that you will inform each other if one of you becomes aware of a child who violates this pact.

- Call the parents whose home is to be used for a party or other event. Make sure they can assure you that no alcoholic beverages or illegal substances will be dispensed. Check out the event yourself to see that adult supervision is in place. If the event is large, offer to help by enhancing the adult supervision.
- Make it easy for your children to leave a place where substances are being used. Discuss in advance how to contact you or another previously designated adult in order to get a ride home. If another adult provides the transportation, be available to talk about the incident when your child arrives home.
- If your child is away from home and under the influence of alcohol or drugs, tell him or her not to drive home or be driven home by a friend. Tell your child that you want him or her to call you and you will pick the child up. Be sure to tell your child there will be no questions or scolding when he or she calls. You will discuss it the next day.

Children Ages 15–17

The many suggestions offered for the previous age groups need to continue, and if they were not initiated at those ages, it is even more imminent to do so now. Continue to praise and encourage your teenage children for all the things they do well and for the positive choices they make. When you are proud of your son or daughter, tell him or her.

Prior to any knowledge that your child may have already started to experiment with alcohol or drugs, I suggest a "no use" rule be a clear expectation that is established in the family. The "no use" rule is clear and reasonable as it simply follows state laws, such as no drinking under the age of twenty-one, no possession or use of illegal drugs, and no illegal actions related to alcohol and drug use. However, another reason for the "no use" rule is the damage alcohol and drugs do to the development of the teenage brain.

To enforce the "no use" rule there must be consequences for breaking the rule, and your children need to know what those consequences are. Logical consequences require some action on your part to help the teenager experience the full impact of his or her behavior. An effective logical consequence is related to the incident. "You were drinking in the car so I am taking the keys away. We had agreed earlier that if you drank while you had use of the car you would lose the privilege of the car keys for a month, so I am now holding you to that agreement."

Older teens have already had to make decisions many times about whether or not to try drinking or using other drugs. To resist peer pressure, teens need more than a general message not to use drugs.

- They need to be warned of the potentially deadly effects of combining drugs.
- They need to hear a parent's assertion that anyone can become a chronic user or an addict and that even nonaddicted use can have serious, permanent consequences.
- They need to be reminded that alcohol and drugs affect the brain and impair judgment, even when used in small doses.
- Because most high school students are future oriented, they may listen to discussions of how alcohol and drugs can sabotage their chances of being admitted to a good college, being accepted by the military, or being hired for certain jobs.

Kids often engage in high-risk behavior when they are under the influence, behaviors they would not normally engage in otherwise. They may exhibit sexual behaviors when they wouldn't have otherwise, they may get in a car with a driver who is under the influence when they wouldn't otherwise, they may be a part of a group that steals a car or breaks into a house when they wouldn't have otherwise. When under the influence one does not make one's best decisions. Many of those decisions will have serious and possibly long-term effects.

- On a long-term basis, drinking and using can affect thinking, problem solving, and motivation.
- Alcohol and other drug consumption during pregnancy has been linked with birth defects in newborns.

> Occasional alcohol or other drug use is a serious matter. A child who may get drunk or high on a drug, even less than once a month, can suffer serious consequences, such as flunking an important test or having a car accident or a heart attack.

Preliminary research indicates that heavy, regular drinking can damage the developing brains of teens and young adults and perhaps destroy brain cells involved in learning and memory.[8]

Alcohol is thought to disrupt brain receptors that form memories. So even if brain cells don't die, a heavy dose of alcohol will garble the ability to encode recent facts and events. Therefore, kids who study all day and drink at night might have trouble getting their facts right on a test the next day.

> Parents profoundly shape the choices their children make about alcohol and drugs.[9]

Educate yourselves. While you may not know what substance was used or consumed, get information that will provide knowledge about the latest drug slang, types of drugs, and methods of drug use now in vogue.

Should your children, adolescent or adult, drink or use, practice tough love. Tough love means letting go of enabling behavior, behavior that makes it easier for your children to avoid the consequences of their behavior.

Choices and Consequences

There need to be clear rules for children and consequences for breaking those rules. Commonly, there are rules that have to do with expectations for dinner, bedtime, curfew, respect for each other, and behavior outside the home. An effective rule is *specific* (after schoolwork is completed, curfew on school nights is 9:00 P.M.), *reasonable* (allows time to be with friends and family and still get a good night's sleep), and *enforceable* (there will be consequences if the rule is not followed).

Discuss ahead the consequences of breaking the rules. The consequences should be reasonable and related to the violation. Whatever the punishment that is settled on, it should not involve new penalties that were not previously discussed before the rule was broken. That would not be fair. Nor should you issue empty threats. It is understandable that you would be angry when family rules are broken, and sharing your feelings of anger, disappointment, or sadness can have a powerfully motivating effect on your child. But since you may be more inclined to say things you do not mean when you are upset, it is best to cool off enough to calmly discuss the consequences.

Help your children understand that they choose the consequences by not adhering to the rules.

When dealing with a teenager, choices can be very helpful. You can offer choices in three specific areas: while addressing a specific behavior, when determining consequences, and when enforcing consequences.

- *Addressing a Specific Behavior.* If your teenager is playing computer games and has not done his homework, give him a choice. Tell him he can do his homework now and have some free time after dinner, or he can wait until after dinner and do his homework then. What does he want to do?
- *Determining Consequences.* If your teenager has come home two hours past her curfew, give her a choice. She can come home two hours early each of the following weekend nights or lose one weekend night. What does she want to do?
- *Enforcing Consequences.* If your teenager is caught with drugs and the other parent hasn't been told yet, give him a choice. He can tell his other parent himself, or you will tell. What does he want to do?

Contrary to some parents' fears, children want you to show you care enough to lay down the law and go to the trouble of enforcing it. Rules about what is acceptable—from curfews to insisting that they call to tell you where they are—make children feel loved and secure. Rules about alcohol or drugs also give them reasons to fall back on when they feel tempted to make bad decisions.

If you are reading all of this and feel you would be the most tyrannical and probably hated parent for following through with these suggestions, you could possibly be reacting to the incredible difference in these suggestions and how you were raised. Certainly if you were raised in a home with little guidance, little structure, and inconsistent supervision, this will seem extreme. If you were raised with unreasonable rigidity, you may think you need to be much more permissive than could be healthy. What is described here is responsible, conscientious parenting. Your job is providing appropriate structure and protection as your children are growing.

Other ways your family history may impact your parenting is if you struggle with issues of the fear of rejection, need for approval, or strong fear of conflict. These issues can cut you down at the knees and are common for people raised in addictive families or other troubled families. If these issues are influencing your ability to provide healthy limit setting and structure, it is vital you find a counselor to help you address how these issues interfere in your parenting skills.

Your children do not need you to be their best friend; they need you to be their best parent.

If you do not enforce the rules, later in life they will be angry with you. Here's how Carmen talks about her expectations of her children:

The most important things my husband and I do that we think will prevent our teenage sons from following our path is to convey clear messages that we won't condone any usage, not while they are living in our home. We keep them involved in many activities, so there is little time for them to get in trouble. We do a lot of what they like rather than just having them fit into our lives. We don't lecture; we are simply a part of their lives. We know who their friends are. If we are suspect about a particular friend, then that friend can be in our lives, in our home, but we limit our sons being in that friend's home, etc. We always know where they are, and what's great is, they are often with us.

Adult Children

If your child is an adult, you are not in a position to have the leverage and influence you would have with a teenager. Should you believe your adult-age child is addicted, remember that addicted people are delusional in their thinking and manipulative. If they can use you in ways to protect them and cover up their behavior, they will. You must remember, if you are seeing signs that they are addicted, you are only seeing the tip of the iceberg. You must trust those signs. Many recovering parents are accused of just "seeing things" or seeing themselves in their child's behavior, which may create self-doubt. If you can objectively identify your child's behaviors, that is the reality. So, if it is helpful, write down what you see and hear.

As a parent who loves your children, it is responsible parenting to

- tell them what you see
- speak specifically about their behavior
- tell them the impact you see their behavior having on you and others close to them
- let them know you are willing to help them locate assistance
- remind them that addiction only gets progressively worse and that you would hope they would get help now

Tell your addicted child this is not a confidential conversation, and you will share your concerns with other significant people in his or her life. This, by the way, is where you may have the greatest influence. Talk to your child's most significant other (i.e., spouse, partner) and explain what you know about addiction. Tell the significant other the nature of your concern regarding your child's behavior. You can offer resources such as Al-Anon, an interventionist, or specific reading material. Be clear with this person that you will not enable him or her or your child. So often a partner or spouse feels alone and angry and questions his or her own reality. This denial is fueled by a need to not believe. Be clear with your reality to both your addicted child and his or her significant other and know you are coming from a place of love.

These suggestions can help you talk to your adult child if you are worried about his or her drug or alcohol use:

- Confront your child with respect, offering choices.
- Do not confront while he or she is under the influence of alcohol or drugs.
- Do not confront your child when you are angry.
- Do not make threats you are not willing to enforce.
- Do not humiliate your child.

- Do not use physical violence or verbal abuse.
- Do not enable. Let your child experience his or her own pain.
- Get support. Addiction is a system disease, and it takes a system to break a system.

Enabling

Enabling is a concept commonly recognized when addressing family members of someone who is addicted, but is relevant to any undesirable behavior and certainly to a child's use of alcohol or drugs, whether or not you believe the child is addicted. Enablers are usually family or friends who take responsibility for the behaviors, feelings, and decisions of the user. Out of love, concern, fear, shame, or a combination of these, enablers react and behave in ways that shield the user from experiencing the consequences of his or her use. Enabling only makes it easier for the person to continue to use.

Teenagers have more enablers in their lives than adults. The average chemically dependent adult might have as many as ten to twelve enablers: family, friends, in-laws, a doctor, boss, co-workers, and maybe the court. A teenager might have fifty to sixty enablers: immediate family, grandparents, uncles, aunts, friends, parents of friends, school personnel, church staff, law enforcement officers, and court personnel.

Enabling is when you make excuses for your children's behavior; when you bail them out of difficulty (rationalizing and denying throughout); and when you don't hold them accountable for their behavior.

Enabling your children is also when you

- lie to your spouse, relatives, or the school about their behavior
- rearrange the family schedule in an attempt to control their behavior
- assume their responsibilities, such as completing homework they didn't do because they were out partying
- move miles away to a different community in an attempt to separate them from friends you believe are a bad influence
- avoid talking about uncomfortable issues, such as saying nothing when you suspect they have been smoking marijuana, because you don't want to act like an untrusting parent

- pretend things are different than they really are by minimizing, rationalizing, and discounting

Enabling behaviors are understandable. They are an attempt to bring order to chaos and comfort to pain. It is much more difficult for parents to stop enabling their children than it is for spouses and friends to stop enabling other adults. For parents (recovering addict and/or codependent parent), codependent issues, such as the need for approval and fear of rejection or anger, are contributors to enabling and critical barriers to healthy parenting.

Should you suspect your teenager or adult child has a problem with alcohol or drugs, I highly suggest you use Al-Anon as a resource. Al-Anon is a self-help, Twelve Step program specifically for family and friends of someone who has a problem with alcohol or drugs. It will offer you support and validation to practice tough love.

Tough Love

Tough love for teens and young adults means the following:

- You do not cover up for them.
- You do not tell lies for them.
- You do not make excuses for them.
- You do not loan them money.
- You do not bribe them with money or presents.
- You do not clean up their messes.
- You tell them how their behavior affects you.
- You intervene and refer for assessment if they are adolescents who continue to use.

Tough love is just that, tough. You want so much to protect your child that you can quickly tap into your own denial and guilt and sometimes become confused about the seriousness of a situation. If your child is using drugs or drinking when he or she is underage, this is serious. If your child is breaking the rules of the family, this is serious. If your child no longer lives at home and is of legal age to drink and is drinking more than occasionally and moderately, this is serious. Children from addictive families are at high risk for addiction because of their genetic vulnerability. While you cannot stop them from drinking or using, you can certainly tell them what you see and practice responsible parenting by not enabling.

Consider for a moment raising a toddler. You didn't carry that toddler everywhere until she was six years of age because you didn't want her to risk falling and being in pain. Had you done that she never would have learned to walk. She wouldn't have learned the basics of needing to step a little higher to climb over an obstacle. It was important that you not get in the way of the development of basic skills for this young child. As that applies to the toddler, it applies to the older child who may be in trouble with drugs or alcohol.

Simply stated, tough love means you allow your children to experience the consequences of their behavior. When you attempt to shield or protect them from their own behavior, you are only protecting the behavior or the addiction.

> **You are not helping your children by rescuing them from negative consequences, you are only rescuing the behavior or the addiction.**

You will come to find your strength by identifying where you have the power to effect change and where you do not. The Serenity Prayer, by Reinhold Niebuhr, is vital. "God, grant me the serenity to accept the things I cannot change, courage to change the things I can, and wisdom to know the difference."

Having said a lot in relatively few pages, I hope I have given you a framework to talk to your children and to influence them positively. In closing, let me remind you of two basic principles:

"First Things First." Don't underestimate the insidiousness of addiction. Without active recovery practices you won't be the parent your children need you to be.

To have a relationship with your children, they need your love and your time—make both a priority.

Appendix

Tracing Addictions on a Family Tree

MOTHER'S SIDE	FATHER'S SIDE
Maternal Grandparents	Paternal Grandparents
Grandmother/Grandfather	Grandmother/Grandfather

_____   _____   _____   _____

Name Aunts with Spouses   Name Aunts with Spouses

_____   _____   _____   _____

Name children   Name children

MOTHER'S SIDE
Name Uncles with Spouses

_____ _____

Name children

_____
_____
_____
_____
_____
_____
_____
_____
_____

FATHER'S SIDE
Name Uncles with Spouses

_____ _____

Name children

_____
_____
_____
_____
_____
_____
_____
_____
_____

PARENTS

2nd Husband (Stepfather)	MOM	DAD	2nd Wife (Stepmother)
_____	_____	_____	_____
_____			_____

Sisters & Brothers (Include Yourself)	Spouse	Children	
_____	_____	_____	_____
		_____	_____
_____	_____	_____	_____
		_____	_____
_____	_____	_____	_____
		_____	_____
_____	_____	_____	_____
		_____	_____
_____	_____	_____	_____
		_____	_____

Notes

Chapter 1: Straight Talk about Addiction and Recovery

1. Grant, B. F. 2000. Estimates of U.S. children exposed to alcohol abuse and dependence in the family. *American Journal of Public Health* 90 (1): 112–115.

2. Schuckit, M. 1998. *Educating yourself about alcohol and drugs*. University of California San Diego: Plenum Trade.

Chapter 2: Breaking the Chain of Addiction

1. Holden, Constance. 2001. Behavioral addictions: Do they exist? *Science* 294 (5544): 980–982.

2. Ibid.

3. Wise, R. A. 1987. The role of reward pathways in the development of dependence. *Journal of Pharmacology and Therapeutics* 35:227–263.

4. Helmuth, Laura. 2001. Beyond the pleasure principle. *Science* 294: 983–984.

Chapter 3: Generational Vulnerability

1. Johnson, S., K. E. Leonard, and T. Jacob. 1989. Drinking, drinking styles and drug use in children of alcoholics, depressives and controls. *Journal of Studies on Alcohol* 50:427–432.

2. Cotton, N. S. 1979. The familial incidence of alcoholism: A review. *Journal of Studies on Alcohol* 40:89–116.

3. Sigvardsson, S., M. Bohman, and C. R. Cloninger. 1996. Replication of the Stockholm adoption study of alcoholism: Confirmatory cross-fostering analysis. *Archives of General Psychiatry* 53:681–687. Pickens, R. W., D. S. Svikis, M. McGue, et al. 1991. Heterogeneity in the inheritance of alcoholism. *Archives of General Psychiatry* 48:19–28.

4. Schuckit, *Educating yourself about alcohol and drugs*.

5. Begleiter, Henri. 2001. For his breakthrough studies on inherited factors in alcoholism in *Hazelden Voice* by Patricia Owen. Butler Center for Research at Hazelden: Center City, Minn. www.hazelden.org/research/person. November 27, 2002.

6. Heath, A. C., K. K. Bucholz, P. A. F. Madden, et al. 1997. Genetic and environmental contributions to alcohol dependence risk in a national twin sample: Consistency of findings in women and men. *Psychology & Medicine* 27:1381–1396.

7. *Alcoholics Anonymous*. 3d ed. 1976. New York: AA World Services, Inc., 58.

Chapter 4: Clarifying the Confusion

1. Helmuth, Beyond the pleasure principle.

Chapter 5: Early Recovery and Making Amends

1. *Alcoholics Anonymous*, 151.

Chapter 7: Creating Healthy Family Traditions

1. Hawkins, D. J., R. F. Catalano, and J. Miller. 1992. Risk and protective factors for alcohol and other drug problems in adolescence and early adulthood: Implications for substance abuse prevention. *Psychological Bulletin* 112 (1): 64–105.

2. Ibid.

3. U.S. Department of Health and Human Services, National Institute of Health, National Institute on Drug Abuse. 1997. *Preventing drug use among children and adolescents: A research-based guide.* Washington, D.C.: U.S. Government Printing Office. NIH Publication No. 97-4212.

4. Henderson, Nan. 1999. *Resiliency in action: What is resiliency?* Alberta, Canada: Alberta Alcohol and Drug Commission.

5. U.S. Department of Health and Human Services, *Preventing drug use among children and adolescents.*

6. Blum, R. W., and P. M. Rinehart. 1997. Monograph. Reducing the risk: Connections that make a difference in the lives of youth. *National Longitudinal Study of Adolescent Health.* Minneapolis: Division of General Pediatrics and Adolescent Health, University of Minnesota.

7. Henderson, *Resiliency in action.*

8. Booth, Alyse. 2001. CASA 2000 teen survey: Teens with "hands-off" parents at four times greater risk of smoking, drinking, and using illegal drugs as teens with "hands-on" parents. New York: National Center on Addiction and Substance Abuse at Columbia University.

Chapter 8: Never Underestimate Your Power as a Parent
1. Washington State Alcohol and Drug Clearinghouse. 2000. *Washington state survey of adolescent health behaviors.* Seattle: Washington State Alcohol and Drug Clearinghouse.
2. U.S. Department of Health and Human Services, *Preventing drug use among children and adolescents.*
3. Grant, B. F., and D. A. Dawson. 1997. Age at onset of alcohol use and its association with DSM-IV alcohol abuse and dependence: Results of the national longitudinal alcohol epidemiological survey. *Journal of Substance Abuse* 9:103 –110.
4. Hawkins, J. D., J. W. Graham, E. Maguin, K. G. Hill, and R. F. Catalano. 1997. Exploring the effects of age of alcohol use initiation and psychosocial risk factors on subsequent alcohol misuse. *Journal of Studies on Alcohol* 58 (3): 208–290.
5. Schweich Handler, Cindy. 1998. *Growing up drug free: A parent's guide to prevention.* Washington, D.C.: U.S. Department of Education, Safe and Drug Free Schools.
6. Dunn, M. E., and M. S. Goldman. 1998. Age and drinking-related differences in the memory organization of alcohol expectancies in 3rd-, 6th-, 9th-, and 12th-grade children. *Journal of Consulting Clinical Psychology* 66 (3): 579–585.
7. Schweich Handler, *Growing up drug free.*
8. Fackelmann, Kathleen. 2000. Teen drinking, thinking don't mix. *USA Today.* 18 October.
9. Schweich Handler, *Growing up drug free.*

About the Author

Claudia Black, Ph.D., is a renowned lecturer, author, and trainer, internationally recognized for both her pioneering and contemporary work with family systems and addictive disorders. Since the mid-1970s Dr. Black's work has encompassed the impact of addiction on young and adult-age children. She has offered models of intervention and treatment related to family violence, multi-addictions, relapse, anger, depression, and women's issues. *Straight Talk from Claudia Black* is her twelfth book. She is most recognized for her early best-selling primer, *It Will Never Happen to Me*, which has more than two million copies in print.

Dr. Black has been a keynote speaker on Capitol Hill in Washington, D.C., and on Parliament Hill in Ottawa, Canada. Her workshops have been presented to an extraordinarily wide array of audiences at military academies, correctional facilities, mental health and addiction treatment conferences, medical schools, and universities.

Dr. Black is the recipient of a number of national awards and is the past chairperson of the National Association for Children of Alcoholics and presently serves on its advisory board. She resides in the Pacific Northwest.

For more information on Dr. Black's other works and her presentation schedule, visit her Web site at www.claudiablack.com or e-mail cblack@nwlink.com.